Happy Holidays Cookbook

Over 75 Quick, Easy and Delicious Thanksgiving Holiday and Thanksgiving Recipes Including Mains, Desserts, Side Dishes, and More

(2020 Edition)

Lindsey Oliver

© **Copyright 2020 All Right Reserved.**

In no way, it is legal to reproduce, duplicate, or transmit any part of this document by other electronic means or printed format. Any recording of this publication is strictly prohibited, and any storage of this material is not allowed unless with written permission from the publisher. All rights reserved.

The information provided herein is stated to be truthful and consistent, in that any liability, regarding inattention or otherwise, by any use or abuse of any policies, processes, or directions contained within is the solitary and complete responsibility of the recipient reader. Under no circumstances will any legal liability or blame be held against the publisher for any reparation, damages, or monetary loss due 10 the information herein, either directly or indirectly.

Legal Notice:

This book is copyright protected. This is only for personal use. You cannot amend, distribute, sell, use, quote, or paraphrase any part of the content within this book without the consent of the author or copyright owner. Legal action will be pursued if it is breached

DISCLAIMER NOTICE:

Please only read the information contained within this document is for educational purposes only. Every attempt has been made 10 to provide accurate, up to date, complete, and reliable information. No warranties of any kind are expressed or implied. Readers acknowledge that the author is not engaged in the rendering of legal, financial, medical, or professional advice.

By reading this document, the reader agrees that under no circumstances are we responsible for any losses, direct or indirect, which are incurred as a result of the use of the information contained in this document, including but not limited to errors, omissions, or any inaccuracies

TABLE OF CONTENTS

CHAPTER 1: INTRODUCTION **8**
    History of Thanksgiving Holidays 10
    Thanksgiving Culinary traditions around the world 11
CHAPTER 2: Instructions/Information **15**
    Understanding the Nutrition Information of any recipe: 20
    Food Preparation times: 22
CHAPTER 3: Main dishes (~30 recipes) **24**
    Recipe 1: Roasted Turkey 25
    Recipe 2: Cola Ham 27
    Recipe 3: Fried Turkey breasts 29
    Recipe 4: Turducken 31
    Recipe 5: Fried Pork Tenderloin 33
    Recipe 6: Creamy Shepherd's Pie 35
    Recipe 7: Garlic-Crusted Pork Tenderloin 37
    Recipe 8: Roasted leg of lamb 39
    Recipe 9: Chicken Paprikash 41
    Recipe 10: Liver cutlets with berry sauce 43
    Recipe 11: Cranberry-Stuffed Turkey Roll 45
    Recipe 12: Chicken with peaches 47
    Recipe 13: Honey-Glazed Pork Ham 49
    Recipe 14: Turkey Meatloaf 51
    Recipe 15: Baked Duck 53
    Recipe 16: Fruit Stuffed Pork Loin 55
    Recipe 17: Chicken with carrots and dates 58
    Recipe 18: Beef Brisket with onion 61
    Recipe 19: Chicken with Olives and nuts 63
    Recipe 20: Smoked salmon rolls with cream cheese 65
    Recipe 21: Pork Pie 67
    Recipe 22: Pork Fajitas 69
    Recipe 23: Pork with orange sauce 71

Recipe 24: Pork with Chimichurri 73
Recipe 25: Beef Teryaki 75
Recipe 26: Chicken curry 77
Recipe 27: Ground beef and sweet potato skillet 79
Recipe 28: Bacon-wrapped fillet mignon 81
Recipe 29: Salmon with orange juice 83
Recipe 30: Baked Barramundi with olives 85

CHAPTER 4: Soups & Salads (~10 recipes) 87

Recipe 31: Chicken and Cheese Soup 88
Recipe 32: Broccoli Soup 90
Recipe 33: Green Asparagus Soup 92
Recipe 34: Mushroom Soup 94
Recipe 35: Carrot Soup 96
Recipe 36: Tomato Soup 98
Recipe 37: Coconut Celery Soup 100
Recipe 38: Beets Salad 102
Recipe 39: Cabbage Salad 104
Recipe 40: Cesar Salad 106

Snacks/Sides (~20 recipes) 108

Recipe 41: Sweet Potato Chips 109
Recipe 42: Cheddar Cheese Crackers 111
Recipe 43: Parsnip Chips 112
Recipe 44: Avocado Hummus 114
Recipe 45: Crispy Roasted Kale 116
Recipe 46: Mashed broccoli 118
Recipe 47: Roasted Radish 120
Recipe 48: Sweet Glazed Carrots 122
Recipe 49: Baba Ghanoush 124
Recipe 50: Red pepper Hummus 126
Recipe 51: Stuffed Peppers 128
Recipe 52: Stuffed Mushrooms 130
Recipe 53: Pork Koftas 132
Recipe 54: Stuffed Potatoes 134
Recipe 55: Beef Fritters 136

Recipe 56: Candied pork rinds 138
Recipe 57: Stuffed Sardines 139
Recipe 58: Salmon Cakes 141
Recipe 59: Scotch Eggs 143
Recipe 60: Spring Rolls 145

Dressings & Dips (~5 recipes) 147

Recipe 61: Spinach dip 148
Recipe 62: Onion dip 150
Recipe 63: Cheese Dip 152
Recipe 64: Chicken and mayonnaise dip 154
Recipe 65: Salad Vinaigrette 155

Desserts (~10 recipes) 157

Recipe 66: Coconut butter dark chocolate bars 158
Recipe 67: Cinnamon dates cookies 160
Recipe 68: Chocolate Truffles 162
Recipe 68: Christmas Log 164
Recipe 69: Medjool Dates Pie 166
Recipe 71: Healthy Dark Chocolate Cake 168
Recipe 72: Macadamia cookies 170
Recipe 73: Cocoa Myffins 172
Recipe 75: Lava Cake 174

Concluding Chapter 176

References: 178

CHAPTER 1: INTRODUCTION

When the holidays are around the corner and you start thinking about the best ideas that can help you enjoy a perfect thanksgiving holiday with your friends and family; what do you usually think of and envision? I would love to enjoy sitting next to the fireplace smelling the flavorful dish, and enjoying the cozy ambiance of the sweet home. For me; thanksgiving is more about sharing the warmth of sumptuous thanksgiving dishes and meals with the people I love and cherish the most.

Only during Thanksgiving, we share each other's dishes; stories with the aromas of various recipes and a large array of homemade foods fillings the air around you; warmth you will never be able to forget. Unfortunately, the excitement and energy you usually start thanksgiving and holidays with, end up with the huge number of guests from family and friends you will have to deal with on this happy occasion.

And instead of enjoying this cheerful occasion, you will find yourself thinking whether your guests will like the meals you have prepared or not and whether you have prepared enough dishes for this occasion. And on this framework, I offer you this Thanksgiving Cookbook that is loaded with a large array of different categories of sumptuous recipes from different countries of the world. And for me, it is the smallest details that matter to me, special twists that I add to every recipe; every touch I put into food, I put with big love. And there is nothing you can express your love through like food you prepare at home.

So if you are looking for more than an ordinary cookbook that will teach you everything you need to know about thanksgiving food and delicious dishes; you have come to the right place and you have picked the best cookbook you can find. And only with the help of this cookbook, you will be able to synchronize everything harmoniously together starting with a few fresh ingredients and you, with your hand, will be able to forget all the stress; headaches any all the exhaustion of cooking in thanksgiving.

So, if you used to be stressed at the thought of cooking and preparing meals during Thanksgiving holidays; worry no more with the help this book provides you with. This cookbook will provide you all the help you need to come up with a beautiful thanksgiving table without feeling any stress and without having to think for endless nights and hours about the dishes that your family will like the most.

This cookbook includes all the solutions to your cooking problems in thanksgiving and carries the relief you are looking for within the recipes you will find in this book. The relief you are looking for can be found within the pages of this book. The recipes contained here all emphasize various flavors and with each recipe, you will learn to value time more because all the recipes you will find within this book will save your time and energy. So, if you are planning for a joyful holiday season; this cookbook is the major key.

Starting from the use of fresh ingredients, roasting different types of vegetables; cinnamon-scented desserts; to perfect-roasted turkeys; this cookbook offers you a large array of incredibly tasty recipes. And before starting to read this cookbook; you should know that the key to a perfect menu is with following the right planning and the best fitting menu. And the key to succeeding and to avoiding any stress is to keep things simple and your dishes organized and flavorful.

History of Thanksgiving Holidays

Celebrating thanksgiving began with a small number of colonists who went out fowling for turkeys; but who found ducks and geese instead. Later; about ninety or so Wampanoag made a big surprising appearance at the gate of the settlement and unnerved the colonist. And over the following days; both groups socialized very well together. The group of the Wampanoag participated with venison; stews fish; shellfish; beer and vegetables;

And since Plymouth had no more than a very few numbers of buildings as well as manufactured goods, most of the people would eat outside while they are sitting on top of the barrels or directly on the ground with their plates in their laps. During those times; men fired guns; they ran races and they drank liquor while they struggled to speak Wampanoag and broken English.

And the colonists of New England were rather accustomed to celebrating the days of holidays of Thanksgivings with days of prayer thanking God for various blessings like the end of the drought and victory. And the U.S Congress decided to proclaim a National Thanksgiving Holiday right upon the enactment of the Constitution.

Indeed; the era of the 19th century was characterized by great American dishes and home cooking in general. And even before proclaiming it a national Holiday; thanksgiving was celebrated throughout the United States with simple family dinners and simple festivities. Pumpkin pie and Turkey started to make an indispensable part of the Thanksgiving menu and it later became a Thanksgiving tradition.

And Thanksgiving Day did not become an official holiday until the domination of the Northerners of the Federal government. And while there are sectional tensions that prevailed during the mid of the 19th century; the popular editor of the Magazine; Godey's Lady's Book Sarah Hale called for a campaign for a national Thanksgiving Day as a way to promote unity amongst people. And Sarah Hale was finally able to win the support of the president of the United States; Abraham Lincoln. And on October the 3rd of 1863; President Lincoln proclaimed the Thursday of November the 26th a National Thanksgiving official celebration Holiday.

Thanksgiving Culinary traditions around the world

When we say Thanksgiving Holidays, we say sumptuous foods and recipes, we say family gatherings and we say incredible atmosphere. And when we say atmosphere, we say lighting fireplace and share the joyful moment with all the family and loved ones. And what is more wonderful is that the Thanksgiving Holiday allows us to enjoy colorful dishes. Besides, it is during the Thanksgiving celebrations that you can smell the varied meals which will invade all the rooms of your house and all the places and which will play a very important role in the reunion of all the members of families and in uniting people.

Traditionally, Thanksgiving Holiday brings together all the members of the family around a table rich in varied and delicious dishes. We find all types of meals on the same table begin with the traditional dish of turkey with chestnuts, chickens, oysters, smoked salmon, snails, hearty Thanksgiving stews and sides served and each Thanksgiving Holiday ends with sweet dessert recipes, melted chocolate, and with the base of butter cream as well as pudding. Each Thanksgiving table features red bright colors to remind us of warm sunshine and green color that indicates hope. So how do we prepare for the Thanksgiving Holiday celebration and what dishes can we cook? Yet, before starting to learn some of the most mesmerizing recipes ever, we have to learn a little about the culinary traditions of different countries around the world.

Thanksgiving holiday dishes in various countries around the world:

Sharing an exceptional Thanksgiving Holiday on the same table and enjoying a warm meal with the family is a joyous moment shared, without exception, in all countries around the world. However, the dishes cooked during thanksgiving vary from country to another as each country has different specific characteristics and culinary specialties. Indeed, desserts are the main feature in some countries while fish and meat are mandatory items in a few other countries. And here is an overview and some examples that will help you to discover the different culinary traditions of Thanksgiving Holidays in some countries:

1. IN FRANCE

Thanksgiving Holiday is a very important occasion in France and the celebration of this holiday dates back thousands of years. This is why the French celebrate luxurious, voluptuous, and fine dishes on this occasion. So, therefore, we will find on every French table truffles, oysters, scallops, caviar, and salmon.

2. IN ITALY

In Italy and precisely in the north of the country, meals cooked at Thanksgiving Holidays are generally plentiful. We start with cheeses, various antipasti, stuffed vegetables, and cold meats. And Italians wouldn't celebrate without the tortellini and the irresistible taste of lasagna and we don't forget to mention that the Italians favor the stuffed pasta. The dishes which consist of meats are generally presented afterward as the Lessa carne. And in the end, we find a very succulent cake made with raisins and citrus fruits.

3. IN SPAIN

Typical dishes from Spain are roast lamb, stuffed turkey, and Buena Noche. And the Spaniards emphasize, precisely, a confectionery composed of almonds, honey, and egg whites. One of the best dishes presented by the Spanish is the Iberian version of nougat.

4. IN QUEBEC

The Meat Pie; or what the Canadians call it tourtière du Lac is the main focus of several cultures and this dish contains a variety of ingredients. There are different versions of tourtière. Besides; stuffed turkey occupies a unique place on our Thanksgiving Holiday table. Stuffed turkey is also known for the simplicity of this recipe, its economy, and this recipe appeals to everyone. Plus, in Quebec, you can use leftover turkey to create a multitude of delicious recipes. Besides, Quebec is characterized by another dish known as ragout and this recipe consists of meatballs and legs and it is accompanied by steamed potatoes. The succulent Yule log is also a dessert preferred by Quebecers in the Thanksgiving holiday party.

5. IN PORTUGAL

Portugal celebrates Thanksgiving Holidays invitingly and generously and traditionally the Portuguese are known for presenting cod croquettes, chorizo sardines, and cod.

6. IN RUSSIA

Russia is a country that is known for the frequency of snow and it is its nostalgic climate that makes the holiday of Thanksgiving Holiday a pleasant occasion in which the winter colors blend with the beauty of the snow. And to celebrate Christmas, the Russians load their tables with vodka and champagne. The Russians serve koulibiac and brioche pie as a starter and salmon or meat for the main course. Beef Stroganov is one of Russia's favorite dishes in the thanksgiving holidays.

7. IN GERMANY

The Thanksgiving Holiday is celebrated by the Germans and especially on December 25 with a variety of dishes. We find as a starter smoked salmon and we find as the main course a roast goose accompanied by apples and red cabbage. The Germans also prepare the stollen; the cake is made with almond cream.

8. IN GREECE

Greece celebrates the holiday of Thanksgiving Holiday with its specified method which manifests itself in the preparation of turkey stuffed with tomato and berries. And during the festivities, the table of Greece is rich in dishes such as melomakarona, made from honey and nuts, kourabiedes, and covered with icing sugar.

9. THANKSGIVING HOLIDAY PARTY IN THE UNITED STATES

The holiday of Thanksgiving is celebrated in the United States by serving roast beef. There isn't a very traditional menu that characterizes America, but the vibe is the most prominent in the United States and it differs from state to state. Table decorations, especially at the White House, are made with the President's Cake and this is a tradition that characterized the United States of the Abraham Lincoln period.

10. TRINIDAD TOBAGO

If you ever visit Trinidad for the Thanksgiving Holiday; you are going to notice the influences of British, Creole, and Indian food. Trinidadians drink sorrel juice during the Thanksgiving Holiday celebration; they drink the hibiscus juice and serve the cream which is made from rum. And in Trinidad, the festivities include black cake which has a British influence and resembles pudding.

CHAPTER 2: Instructions/Information

Cooking is an art and not a duty and only those who understand this value and believe in it can come up with incredibly delicious recipes for any occasion. Cooking; especially on a special occasion; like Thanksgiving Holidays can be quite challenging for the first time if you don't know some basic cooking tips. And for this reason; I have written this chapter for you and provided you with the most useful tips and through different charts that can lead you through your cooking journey.

- **Food Preparation is the major key:**

Cooking starts with good preparation of the right tools, cooking utensils as well as ingredients. Make sure to purchase all the ingredients that you will need; then make a checklist of the types of equipment and the tools that you need to use. Besides, purchasing all the ingredients that you need to cook and making a checklist as well as proper and perfect preparation is considered as one of the most important keys that can separate the professional cook from the newbie.

- **Baking dishes:**

Whenever you bake; make sure that all your ingredients are already pre-measured. Besides, the temperature is a very important determiner in the process of baking. You should always follow the temperature recommendations included within each recipe. And the process of baking should be followed in a precise way. Furthermore; under-mixing and over-mixing can also the taste of your dish. Always make sure not to overcrowd your oven if you are using and make sure not to open the oven very often.

- **Food hygiene**

Whenever you prepare for cooking, always make sure to wear clean clothes and to put on an apron whenever you cook and enter your kitchen. Besides; you should wash your hands very well before and after the process of cooking, especially after working with raw meat and with any other food ingredients and items.

Make sure to pull your hair back so that you can prevent any loose hair from coming in contact with your food or food items. Besides; you should wash the meat; the poultry; the vegetables; the fruits and any ingredients you want to use in cooking. In addition to this; you should avoid handling cooking when you feel ill or sick.

- **Frying food:**

Frying is known for being one of the most popular cooking procedures that people use all over the world. Dry and cool places are also considered as the best storage places as far as frying is concerned. Keep in mind that it is not advisable to fry salted or moist products. You should also fry your food ingredients in small portions so that the oil won't be cooling quickly. Moreover; frying pans should be preheated very well.

- **On cooking vegetables and fresh ingredients:**

It is usually advisable to scrub your fresh ingredients and vegetables rather than peeling everything very well. Most of the nutrients can be found in the skin of the fruits and vegetables; so make sure to steam your vegetables or to microwave it rather than boiling vegetables.

- **Finish up with a pleasant food presentation**

With a beautiful presentation, you would be able to entice any person to taste the food you have prepared. It is also a good idea to beautifully decorate your dishes; but only with edible food ingredients. You can also use similar food ingredients that are prevalent in your dish for garnishing. Indeed, you can create for example chocolate curls so that you can top a sumptuous chocolate cake.

- **Grilling food**

Whenever you grill food, you should remember that the marinade makes the key factor of a good grilled fish. All you need to do is to place a generous amount of marinade to the food ingredients that you are going to grill. Besides, a good amount of coal can also add to the quality of the food. And it is with these important and basic tips that you can ensure to make your way to a satisfying meal. And in addition to these cooking tips; there are many other cooking basics you need to know so that you cook like a professional from the first time; like learning the cooking time for each ingredient you use. And on this framework, here are some charts that can help you cook like a pro.

Ingredients	temperature Gas °C °F	Cooking	Per pound (kg) of meat + extra mins.
Chicken and poultry	4 to 5 180 350	Medium Well done	19/lb (41/kg) +20 mins
Beef	4-5 180 350 4-5 180 350 4-5 180 350	Rare Medium Well done	20/lb (45/kg) +20 mins 25/lb (55/kg) +20 mins 30/lb (66/kg) +30 mins
Pork	4-5 180 350 4-5 180 350	Medium Well done	30/lb (66/kg) +30 mins 35/lb (77/kg) +35 mins
Lamb	4-5 180 350 4-5 180 350	Medium Well done	25/lb (55/kg) +25 mins 30/lb (66/kg) +30 mins
Mutton	4 180 350 10 250 500 4 180 350	Method 1 Method 2	40-45/lb (88-99/kg) First 15 mins, then 25-30/lb (55-66/kg)
Wild Venison	8 230 451	Can be marinated before	14 to 20/lb
Boar meat	7 220 425 6 200 400	Marinate 2 to 8 hours before cooking.	10; 15 to 20 mins/lb (34-45/kg)

- **Make sure to prepare everything ahead of time:**

To be able to prepare the various dishes that you have prepared ahead of time and to keep everything ready for your guests on Thanksgiving; you should be prepared perfectly.

- **Make sure to assemble rather more than cook**

Always make sure to choose as simple spreads as you can; you may also think about appetizers that may require no cooking, but rather stacking or wrapping or using simple ingredients.

Make cooking in thanksgiving a familiar affair:

When you feel that things are becoming overwhelming for you and you feel that you are missing the true spirit of the holiday season; stop doing everything by yourself.

Using Edible "Table-scapes"

If you favor fancy tables for holiday meals; you should consider combining appetizers with decorations. Indeed; filling glistening glassware with shrimp cocktails; breadsticks, holiday candies, or shrimp cocktails will bring the festivity spirit to any table.

- **Some tricks that are used to save your time during Thanksgiving Holidays:**

To save your time during the Holidays; you will find in this book seventy-five delicious recipes that you need to offer your family a stress-free feast both to your friends and family. And you will also find help in this book from recipe instructions; checklist for ingredients you generally use for Thanksgiving; serving times; and everything you need to know about cooking. Besides; each recipe is accompanied by a picture that will simplify understanding it for you. And combined with all the elements of any recipe needs; you will find calculated the nutrition information needed with each recipe. And here are some additional tips that you will need to come up with a delicious meal on Thanksgiving Holidays. Besides, here are some additional pieces of advice that you can follow to reduce your time in the kitchen and that can save your energy. You can also start planning as early as possible for the Thanksgiving Holidays and you may also prepare some sides and make menus.

Make menus for the meals you will be hosting, and anticipate any dishes that you may need to bring to others' festivities. Make a detailed list of all the ingredients that you will need over the holidays, including those for baked goods, and it is better to adjust the amounts for increased portion sizes. Start a month or more ahead of time, and slowly chip away at your holiday style of cooking. Furthermore; in this book; each of the recipes is created in a way to simplify your meal preparation as a whole. And while some dishes can be make-ahead; where all you need to do is to warm up before serving each recipe; some other recipes included in this cookbook need no more than ten to fifteen minutes of preparation time. And this means that you will be able to enjoy all the flavors of the Thanksgiving Holiday.

So are you ready to enjoy some of the most enjoyable and delicious meals of Thanksgiving without feeling stressed or depressed by spending an enjoyable time with your loved ones; get ready to read the recipes to come? And here are some abbreviations that can help you in the kitchen:

- **Useful food Abbreviations:**

1 oz = 1 ounce fl oz = fluid 1 ounce 1tsp = 1 teaspoon 1tbsp = 1 tablespoon 1 ml = 1 milliliter 1 c = 1 cup 1 pt = 1 pint 1qt = 1 quart 1 gal = 1 gallon 1L = 1 liter

Understanding the Nutrition Information of any recipe:

- **Explaining Nutrition**

Nutrition can be defined as the way food affects our health and overall body condition. And the food is very important for us and our lives as it provides us with the vital nutrients our body needs to survive. Besides; nutrients help our body stay healthy and function very well. Food is also comprised of many macronutrients, including carbohydrates; fat, and proteins. And not only food provides our body with the calories it needs as energy, but it also plays an important role in maintaining our health. Food is made of nutrients, carbohydrates; fats, vitamins, minerals, and more. Besides, food supplies us with phytochemicals and micronutrients that don't provide us with calories that can serve a large array of functions to help ensure that our body operates very well.

- **Explaining what Macronutrients are:**

1. *Calories*

Calories usually provide a proportional measure of how much energy we can get from one serving of a certain type of food. Let us suppose that there are 200 calories in one serving of stew; four servings would be 800 calories.

To maintain or to achieve healthy body weight, you should balance the number of calories you drink and eat with the number of calories your body uses. And 2,000 calories per day is known for being the general guide we can use for nutrition. And nutrition may differ based on the sex, the height, the sex, and the level of physical activity.

Note: The number of servings you consume per day can determine the number of calories you eat. Eating more calories than our body needs may result in obesity.

- **Nutrients to get less of Saturated Fat, Sodium, and Added Sugars.**

Saturated fat, sodium, and added sugars are nutrients listed on the label that may be associated with adverse health effects – and Americans generally consume too much of them, according to the recommended limits for these nutrients. They are identified as nutrients to get less of. Eating too much-saturated fat and sodium, for example, is associated with an increased risk of developing some health conditions, like cardiovascular disease and high blood pressure. Consuming too much-added sugars can make it hard to meet important nutrient needs while staying within calorie limits.

- **Nutrients to get more of Dietary Fiber, Vitamin D, Calcium, Iron, and Potassium.**

Vitamin D, dietary fiber, potassium, and iron are nutrients that are present in any recipe and that you can see labeled on any product you purchase. Eating a diet that is high in Vitamins D; iron; potassium and calcium can greatly reduce any risk of developing illnesses and especially anemia; high blood pressure and osteoporosis. So it is important to read each nutrition label with each recipe that is provided to you in this cookbook if you want to stay healthy and enjoy the Thanksgiving holidays without any health issues.

Note:

Always keep in mind that you can use the nutrition information you will see with each recipe to help you determine better your dietary needs and to choose food that contains the nutrients you want and need. Besides, the nutrition information can help you determine your daily limit of the calories your body needs.

Food Preparation times:

Generally speaking, the amount of time we spend on preparing food and cooking can have important implications for the quality of our diet and our health in general. Yet very little is known about how food is related to time use. Knowing the prep time allows us to strategically create a plan for our week; a plan for what we will eat and how we can prepare the food in advance to save us time and energy and to offer you more time to spend with your family on Thanksgiving.

Prep time can reduce the stress for us and knowing the amount of time we will be spent in the kitchen during Thanksgiving can assure having a meal ready on time.

What should I do during the prep time?

Always determine what you are going to buy versus what you are going to prepare from ingredients. And according to general recipe rules; the general preparation time should include only the time you need to follow the steps that are included in the steps and method instructions. And the preparation time doesn't include the time you spend in chopping or in measuring ingredients.

Thanksgiving ingredients Checklist:

Coming up with a nice big Thanksgiving meal is all about being organized and about preparing a strategy. And whether it is your first time to host a Thanksgiving dinner or not; you should make sure that everything is going to be perfect and that all your dishes are presented beautifully.

So to help you start; here is the thanksgiving ingredients checklist that you will need to be relying on. And you should keep in mind that everything needs to be purchased ahead of time. And to make it easier for you; here is the recapitulation menu of ingredients you need for 6 to 8 people:
- Cranberry sauce
- Baked sweet potatoes
- Green bean casserole
- Raw veggie tray and Pickle
- Roast turkey
- Pumpkin pie
- Homemade dressing
- Cornbread or brown and serve rolls

For the groceries:

- 1012 lbs; Frozen Turkey
- 3 lbs of Onions
- 1Large bunch of Celery
- 1 lb of carrots
- 1 Head of garlic
- 1 loaf of sliced Italian bread of French bread
- 7 Eggs
- 1 lb of Butter
  - 2Bags of fresh cranberries
  - 1 lb of sweet potatoes, large fresh
  - Large Potatoes, large baking
  - 2 packages of 1 pound each of Green beans, regular cut frozen
  - 2 Pound of Mushrooms, fresh
  - 1 quart of Milk
  - 1 can of French fried onion rings
  - 1 can of 115 oz of plain pumpkin
  - A Prepared frozen pie crust
  - 1 can of 1 ½ oz of Evaporated milk
  - 2 Pounds of apples, tart baking
  - 1 Can of spray Whipped cream, or of Vanilla ice cream
  - Veggies: Olives; pickles, radishes, pepperoncini, green onions, etc.
  - Serve rolls
  - Cornbread
  - Beer, wine, coffee

CHAPTER 3: Main dishes (~30 recipes)

Recipe 1: Roasted Turkey

(Prep time: 15 Minutes|Cook Time: 3-4 Hours| Servings: 6-7)

Ingredients:

- 1 Whole turkey of about 12 to 14 pounds; with the giblets and necks removed
- 1 Pinch of kosher salt
- Freshly ground black pepper
- 1 Onion, cut into thin wedges
- 1 Bunch of thyme
- 1 Small handful of fresh rosemary sprigs
- 1 Small handful of sage leaves
- 1 Head of crossed wised halved garlic
- ½ Cup of melted butter
- 2 Cups of chicken broth

Instructions:

1. Start by positioning the rack in the lower third part of your oven and preheat your oven to a temperature of about 450°F

2. Pat the turkey dry with clean paper towels and season the cavity generously with the salt and ground pepper.
3. Stuff the cavity of the turkey with the onion, the thyme, the rosemary, the sage, and the garlic.
4. Tie the legs together with kitchen twine; then tuck the wingtips of the turkey under the body.
5. Brush the butter all over the turkey; then season very well with pepper and salt
6. Place the turkey breast with the side up over a roasting rack in a large pan; then pour the chicken broth in this pan and transfer to the oven
7. Reduce the heat to a temperature of about 350°F
8. Baste every about 30 to 45 minutes with the baked juices that are in the bottom of your pan, and roast for about 3 to 4 hours
9. The inner temperature of the meat should be about 165°F
10. Serve and enjoy your dish!

Nutrition Information

Calories: 177, Fat: 8.4g, Carbohydrates: 0 g, Dietary Fiber: 0g, Protein: 24.3g

Recipe 2: Cola Ham

(Prep time: 15 Minutes|Cook Time: 6-4 Hours| Servings: 6-7)

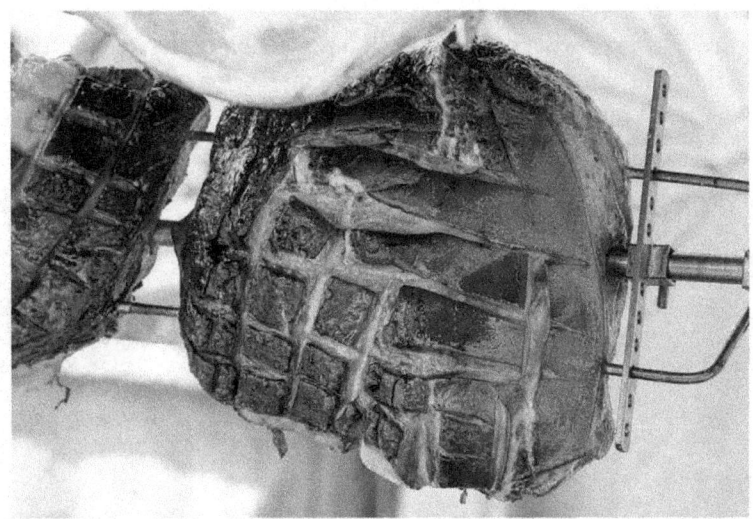

Ingredients:

- ½ Cup of brown sugar (light or dark packed)
- 1 Teaspoon of dry mustard or about 1 heaping tablespoon of Dijon mustard
- ¼ Cup of dark cola
- 1 Ham of about 4 to 5 pounds bone-in, fully cooked or about 3 to 5 pounds of boneless ham
- Whole cloves

Instructions:

1. Gather all your ingredients.
2. In a bowl; mix the brown sugar and the mustard; then stir to blend your ingredients
3. Moisten the mixture with enough cola to make a smooth paste. Reserve the remaining cola and set the mustard-sugar paste aside.
4. With a sharp knife; score the ham with a sharp knife, score the ham with shallow slashes in a diamond pattern.

5. Rub the ham with the mustard-sugar paste mixture; then insert a clove in each of the intersections of the diamond pattern
6. Place the ham in a slow cooker; then add in the remaining quantity of cola
7. Cover the slow cooker and cook on HIGH for about 1 hour; then turn the heat to low and cook for about 6 to 8 hours
8. You can use a thermometer to check the doneness of the meat; 140°F for fully cooked
9. If desired, insert a whole clove in each intersection of the diamond pattern.
10. Baste the ham with the cooking juices an hour before the meat is done
11. Remove from the Crockpot; then let rest for about 15 minutes
12. Serve and enjoy!

Nutrition Information

Calories: 401, Fat: 15g, Carbohydrates: 23 g, Dietary Fiber: 1g, Protein: 41g

Recipe 3: Fried Turkey breasts

(Prep time: 10 Minutes|Cook Time: 30 minutes| Servings: 4-5)

Ingredients:

- 1 Turkey breast of about 3 to 3 1/2 pounds of turkey breast
- 3 Tablespoons/45 mL of Cajun turkey seasoning
- ½ Cup/120 mL of Cajun turkey injection
- 1 to 2 gallons of oil

Instructions:
1. Gather your ingredients.
2. Put the turkey breast into a pot if you are going to fry it; then add in enough water to cover the breast without 3 inches to leave spared
3. Remove the chicken breast; then measure the water that you need to cover the breast
4. Dump out any water; then dry the pan very well with clean paper towels.
5. Pat the chicken dry then trussed breast and part with clean paper towels

6. Coat all over with the Cajun turkey seasoning; then cover with a plastic wrap and set aside altogether for about 15 to 20 minutes.

7. Meanwhile, heat the oil to about 350°F; you can use a thermometer to test; then lower the seasoned breast into the oil and use gloves to protect yourself from any risk of splashing

8. Fry the chicken breast to about 3 minutes per pound; this means that a 3-pound breast will take about 14 minutes; the internal temperature should be about 170 to 175°F

9. Carefully remove from the oil and place over a paper towel-lined with a cutting board. Then let the breast drain for about 5 to 7 minutes

10. Carve into slices of ½ inch each; then serve and enjoy with your favorite side dishes!

Nutrition Information

Calories: 166, Fat: 6g, Carbohydrates: 0g, Dietary Fiber: 2g, Protein: 25g

Recipe 4: Turducken

(Prep time: 20 Minutes|Cook Time: 5 Hours| Servings: 5)

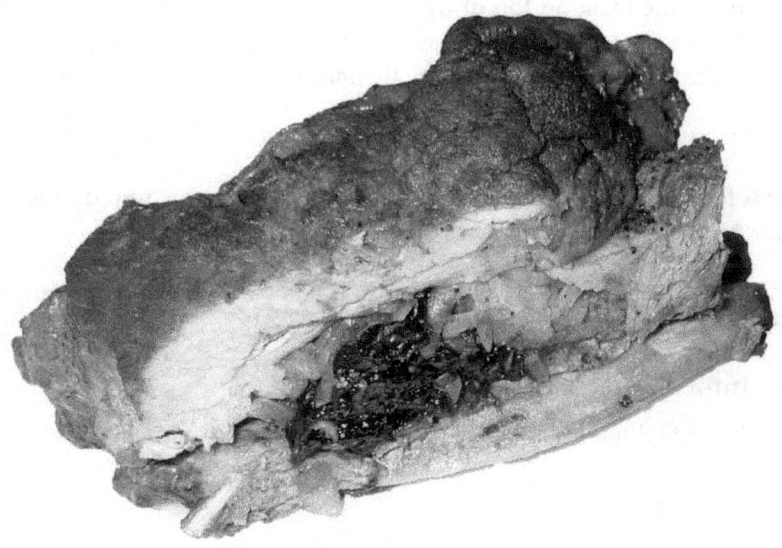

Ingredients:

- 1 Whole chicken of about 3 pounds, boned
- 1 Pinch of salt
- 1 Pinch of pepper to taste
- 1 Pinch of Creole seasoning to taste
- 1 Boned duck of about 4 pounds
- 1 Turkey of about 16 pounds; boned

Instructions:

1. Preheat your oven to a temperature of 375 degrees F; then lay the boned chicken with the skin-side down over a platter; then season with 1 pinch of salt, 1 pinch of pepper, and with the Creole seasoning.

2. Lay the duck skin with the skin down over the top of the chicken and season with salt and pepper; then add Creole seasoning

3. Cover and refrigerate; then lay the boned turkey with the skin-side over a flat service

4. Cover all with a layer of sausage and oyster dressing; then push the dressing into the wing and the leg cavities so that they look to have bones with them

5. Now place the duck on top of the turkey with the skin-side down and cover it with one layer of cold dressing and with the help of an assistant, bring all the edges of the turkey with the skin up; then fasten together with toothpicks

6. Put the turducken with the breast up in a large roasting pan

7. Roast for about 4 hours covered and for about 1 hour uncovered; then check the inner temperature of the meat; it should register about 165°F

8. Check the turducken every about few hours to baste; then remove any excess of liquid.

Nutrition Information
Calories: 298.6, Fat: 12g, Carbohydrates: 15.9g, Dietary Fiber: 1.7g, Protein: 29.8g

Recipe 5: Fried Pork Tenderloin

(Prep time: 10 Minutes|Cook Time: 20 minutes| Servings: 3-4)

Ingredients:

- 2 Finely chopped garlic cloves, about 1 tablespoon
- 1 Tablespoon of finely chopped fresh sage
- 1 and ¼ teaspoons of coarse salt
- ¼ Teaspoon freshly ground pepper
- 1 Tablespoon of olive oil
- 1 Pork tenderloin about 1 and ¼ pounds, tied with
- a kitchen twine
- 1 tablespoon of vegetable oil

Instructions:

1. Preheat the oven to a temperature of about 400 degrees; then stir all together with the garlic, the sage, the salt, the pepper, and the olive oil in a bowl; and rub the mixture all over the pork.

2. Heat a large and heavy pan over medium-high heat; then add in the vegetable oil and add the pork and sauté for about 4 minutes

3. Transfer the pan to the oven; then roast the pork for about 20 minutes while turning from time to time

4. Transfer the pork to a cutting board; then tent with a foil; then let rest for about 10 minutes

5. Serve and enjoy!

Nutrition Information

Calories: 432, Fat: 11g, Carbohydrates: 0.9g, Dietary Fiber: 1.g, Protein: 25g

Recipe 6: Creamy Shepherd's Pie

(Prep time: 15 Minutes|Cook Time: 25 minutes| Servings: 5)

Ingredients:

- 3 tbsp of butter or canola oil divided
- ½ finely diced onion
- 2 large peeled and finely diced carrots
- 1 Stalk of celery; finely diced
- ½ Teaspoon of minced garlic
- 1 tbsp of all-purpose flour
- 1 and ½ cups of chicken broth
- 1 Cup of frozen peas
- 2 Cups of cooked chopped turkey
- 1 Pinch of salt and 1 pinch of pepper
- ½ tsp of dried thyme
- 3 cups of mashed potatoes

Instructions:

1. Heat your oven to a temperature of about 375 degrees F

2. In an oven-safe skillet, melt about 1 tbsp of butter over medium-high heat; then add in the onion; the carrots and cook for about 15 to 20 minutes; then add the garlic and cook for about 1 minute

3. Add in one additional tablespoon of canola oil or of butter to the cooked vegetables; then add in the flour and stir until your ingredients are very well combined

4. Pour in the broth and stir for about 3 to 4 minutes; then stir in the peas and the turkey and cook for about 3 minutes

5. Season with 1 pinch of salt and 1 pinch of pepper; then add the thyme

6. Top with the mashed potatoes and dab with the remaining butter or brush with about 1 tbsp of canola oil.

7. Bake for about 20 minutes, or until the potatoes are heated through very well

Nutrition Information

Calories: 255, Fat: 9g, Carbohydrates: 32g, Dietary Fiber: 4g, Protein: 11g

Recipe 7: Garlic-Crusted Pork Tenderloin

(Prep time: 8 Minutes|Cook Time: 19 minutes| Servings: 3-4)

Ingredients:

- 2 Finely chopped garlic cloves
- 1 tablespoon of finely chopped fresh sage
- 1 and ¼ teaspoons of coarse salt
- ¼ Teaspoon of freshly ground pepper
- 1 Tablespoon of olive oil
- 1 Pork tenderloin of about 1 and ¼ pounds; tied with a kitchen twine
- 1 Tablespoon of vegetable oil

Instructions:

1. Preheat your oven to a temperature of about 400°F.

2. Stir all together with the garlic, the sage, the salt, the pepper, and the olive oil in a bowl; then rub the mixture all over the pork.

3. Heat a large and heavy sauté pan over medium-high heat; then add in the vegetable oil; the pork, and sauté for about 4 minutes

4. Transfer the pan to the oven; then roast the pork while turning it from time to time until a thermometer registers about 145°F; about 19 minutes

5. Transfer the pork to a cutting board; then tent with a foil, and let rest for about 10 minutes before slicing the meat

6. Serve and enjoy your dish!

Nutrition Information

Calories: 209, Fat: 10.3g, Carbohydrates: 0.6g, Dietary Fiber: 0.1g, Protein: 26.8g

Recipe 8: Roasted leg of lamb

(Prep time: 10 Minutes|Cook Time: 30 minutes| Servings: 4-5)

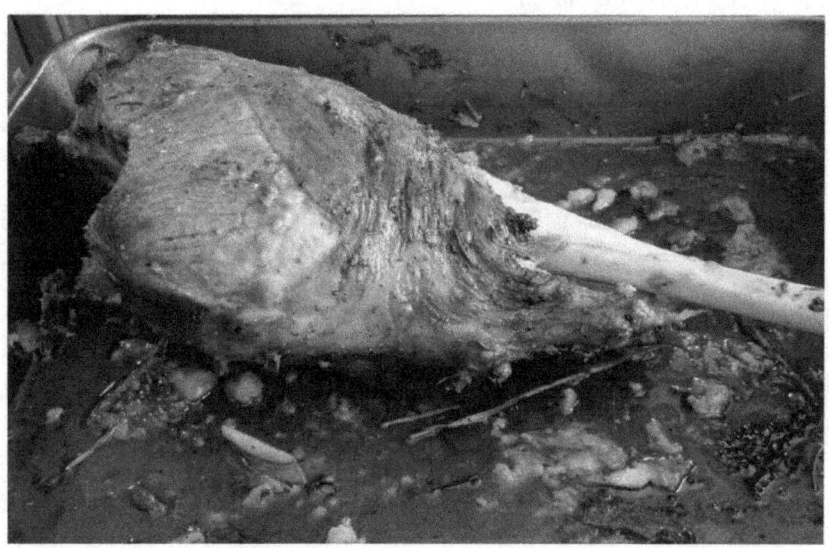

Ingredients:

- A leg of lamb of about 5 pounds
- 3 Garlic cloves divided
- 3 Tablespoons of lemon juice (fresh)
- 2 Tablespoons of fresh rosemary (or about 2 teaspoons of dried rosemary)
- 1 tablespoon of fresh thyme
- 1 Teaspoon of kosher salt
- ¼ Teaspoon of freshly ground black pepper

Instructions:

1. Start by gathering your ingredients; then preheat your oven to a temperature of about 325°F

2. Place a rack in a large roasting pan; then pat the lamb dry with clean paper towels and remove any layer of fat with a sharp knife; then trim any excess
3. Peel the garlic and slice into thin slivers and set it aside
4. Make tiny slits of about 1 inch of dept over the surface of the roast; then insert the garlic slivers into the slits
5. Rub the lamb meat with the lemon juice.
6. Chop the rosemary and thyme; then combine the minced garlic with the herbs; ¼ teaspoon of freshly ground black pepper;1 teaspoon of salt and rub the garlic very well over the meat
7. Put the roast with the fat side up on the rack onto the prepared roasting pan
8. Insert a meat thermometer into the thickest part of the lamb and roast in a preheated oven for about 30 minutes per pound until the thermometer reads about 145°F
9. Once done, remove the roast to a platter and let it rest for about 15 minutes before carving it
10. Serve and enjoy your dish!

Nutrition Information

Calories: 219, Fat: 14g, Carbohydrates: 0 g, Dietary Fiber: 0 g, Protein: 22g

Recipe 9: Chicken Paprikash

(Prep time: 6 Minutes|Cook Time: 20 minutes| Servings: 4)

Ingredients:

- 2 to 2 1/2 pounds of chicken pieces, legs, and thighs
- 1 Pinch of salt
- 2 to 3 Tbsp of unsalted butter
- 2 Pounds of yellow onions
- 1 Pinch of ground black pepper to taste
- 2 Tbsp of sweet paprika
- 1 teaspoon of hot paprika or cayenne
- 1 cup of chicken broth
- ½ Cup of sour cream

Instructions:

1. Season the chicken pieces very well and let sit at room temperature
2. Prepare the onion by slicing it; then brown the chicken pieces in a large sauté over a medium-high heat; then melt in the butter
3. When the butter heats up; pat the chicken dry with clean paper towels; then place it with the skin down into the pan
4. Cook the chicken for about 4 to 5 minutes per side; then turn over and cook for about two additional minutes
5. Remove the chicken pieces and cook for about 4 to 5 minutes on one side; then turn over the other side and cook for about 2 to 3 minutes
6. Remove the chicken from the pan; then add the sliced onions to the sauté pan and sauté for about 7 minutes
7. Add in the paprika and 1 pinch of black pepper and stir; then let cook for about 1 minute
8. Pour the chicken broth over the onions; then cover a cook and scrape any brown bits from the bottom of the pan
9. Nestle the chicken pieces into the pan and top with the onions
10. Cover and cook on a low heat for 20 minutes
11. When the chicken is perfectly cooked through; remove your pan from the heat and remove the chicken, and let the pan cool for about one minute then stir in the sour cream slowly and add salt
12. Add the sour cream to the chicken paprikash in the pan
13. Serve and enjoy your dish!

Nutrition Information
Calories: 146.4, Fat: 4.8g, Carbohydrates: 6.1 g, Dietary Fiber: 0.8 g, Protein: 19g

Recipe 10: Liver cutlets with berry sauce

(Prep time: 5 Minutes|Cook Time: 10 minutes| Servings: 4-5)

Ingredients:

- 3 to 4 liver cutlets
- 1/2 Pound of raspberries, blackberries, and currants
- 2 Tablespoons of raspberry vinegar
- 2 Tablespoons of honey
- The zest of a small orange or the zest of a large ½ orange
- The zest of ½ lemon
- 1 pinch of salt
- 1 pinch of pepper

Instructions:

1. Start by pouring the honey into a medium saucepan and over low heat, caramelize the honey

2. Deglaze the saucepan with the raspberry vinegar; then add the lemon and orange zest with the red fruit mixture

3. Mix very well and cook the mixture until you get a nice texture of raspberry and red fruit jam.

4. Remove your pan from the heat and leave it aside to cool it down

5. Heat the pan without any fat, then cook the cutlets for one minute on each side, then salt and pepper the cutlets and the pan-fried

6. Transfer the escalopes and the pan-fried to plates and serve with the raspberry and red berry jam

Nutrition Information

Calories: 287, Fat: 4g, Carbohydrates: 27 g, Dietary Fiber: 2 g, Protein: 35g

Recipe 11: Cranberry-Stuffed Turkey Roll

(Prep time: 15 Minutes|Cook Time: 60 minutes| Servings: 5)

Ingredients:

- 1 Package of 12 ounces of herb-seasoned bread stuffing mix
- 2 Turley breasts with the bone and skin removed
- 1 Cup of chopped pecans
- 2 Packages of 8 ounces of dried, sweetened cranberries
- 2 tablespoons of olive oil
- 6 leaves of lettuce
- ½ cup of pecan halves

Instructions:

1. Preheat your oven to a temperature of about 350°F (175 degrees C).

2. Prepare the stuffing mix according to the directions on the package; then set it aside to cool down

3. Butterfly the breasts open with a sharp knife; then place each of the breasts between two sheets of waxed paper; flatten with a mallet

4. Spread the prepared stuffing to about ¼ inch of the edge of each of the breasts; then sprinkle each with the dried cranberries and the chopped pecans

5. Reserve some of the cranberries to garnish with; then roll up in a jellyroll style starting with the longer end

6. Tuck in the ends and tie in the sections with a string; 4 sections around the middle and a section all along the roll to secure both ends

7. Heat the olive oil in a large iron skillet over medium-high heat; then carefully sauté the rolls on all the sides

8. Place the skillet in the oven; then bake in a preheated oven at a temperature of about 350°F for about 1 hour

9. Set the rolls aside for about 15 minutes to cool before removing the string; then slice into circles of about ½ inch each

10. Serve on a platter bed of lettuce; then garnish with the remaining pecan and the dried cranberries.

11. Enjoy your dish!

Nutrition Information
Calories: 369.2, Fat: 18.4g, Carbohydrates: 28g, Dietary Fiber: 2.7g, Protein: 23.2g

Recipe 12: Chicken with peaches

(Prep time: 10 Minutes|Cook Time: 15 minutes| Servings: 4)

Ingredients:

- ½ Tablespoon of extra-virgin olive oil
- 1 Tablespoon of grass-fed butter
- 4 Pieces of chicken legs and thighs
- 1 Pinch of salt and 1 pinch of freshly ground black pepper
- ½ Cup of almond flour
- 2 Peaches, chopped into wedges
- 1 Tomato, chopped into wedges
- 2 Thinly sliced red onions
- 2 Diced garlic cloves
- ¼ cup white wine
- ¼ Cup of chopped fresh basil

Instructions:

1. Preheat your oven to a temperature of about 400°F.
2. Heat a large cast-iron skillet over a medium heat; then add in the olive oil and the grass fed butter to the hot pan.

3. Season the chicken with 1 pinch of salt and 1 pinch of pepper
4. Dredge each piece of the chicken into the flour
5. Add the dredged chicken to the pan and cook for about 8 minutes
6. Remove the chicken from the pan
7. Add the peaches to the pan and sear for about 6 to 8 minutes
8. Remove the peaches from the pan
9. Repeat the same process from the tomatoes; then remove from the pan
10. Add the red onions to the pan and sauté until it becomes tender for about 4 to 5 minutes.
11. Add the garlic and cook for about 1 additional minute
12. Deglaze the pan with the wine; then return the chicken to the pan and cook for 1 additional minute
13. Transfer the pan to the oven and roast for about 10 minutes
14. Add the tomatoes and the peaches to the pan and cook for about 3 to 5 additional minutes
15. Garnish with the basil; the serve and enjoy!

Nutrition Information

Calories: 271, Fat: 10g, Carbohydrates: 2g, Dietary Fiber: 2.1g, Protein: 25g

Recipe 13: Honey-Glazed Pork Ham

(Prep time: 15 Minutes|Cook Time: 60 minutes| Servings: 5)

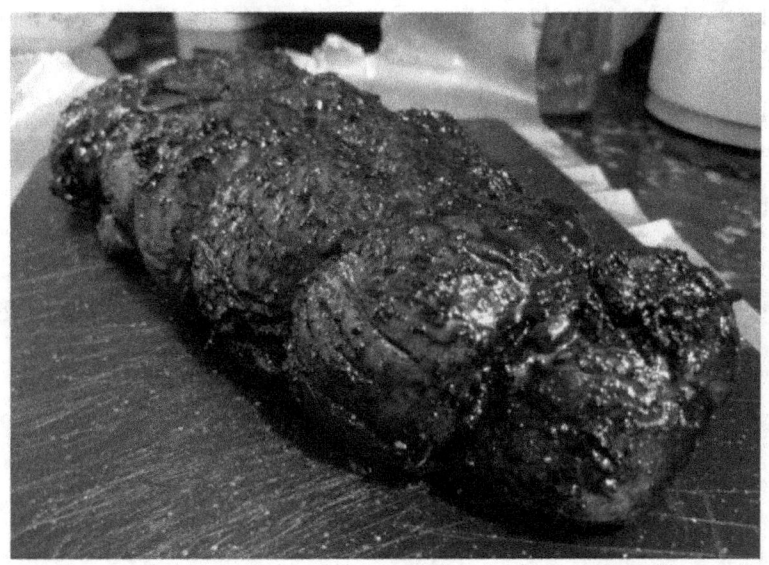

Ingredients:

- 1 fully cooked ham of about 10 pounds
- 1 and ¼ cups of packed dark brown sugar
- ⅓ Cup of pineapple juice
- ⅓ Cup of honey
- ⅓ Large orange; zested and juiced
- 2 Tablespoons of Dijon mustard
- ¼ teaspoon of ground cloves

Instructions:

1. Preheat your oven to a temperature of about 325 degrees F

2. Place the ham in a roasting pan; then combine the sugar, the pineapple juice, the honey, the orange juice, the Dijon mustard, and the ground cloves in a saucepan and bring to a boil

3. Reduce the heat, and let simmer for about 5 to 10 minutes; then set aside

4. Bake the ham in a preheated oven uncovered for about 2 hours; then remove the ham from the oven, and brush with the glaze.

5. Bake for about 30 to 45 minutes; then brush with the ham and with the glaze every about 10 minutes.

6. Let cool for about 5 minutes; then serve and enjoy your dish!

Nutrition Information

Calories: 369.2, Fat: 18.4g, Carbohydrates: 28g, Dietary Fiber: 2.7g, Protein: 23.2g

Recipe 14: Turkey Meatloaf

(Prep time: 6 Minutes|Cook Time: 60 minutes| Servings: 6)

Ingredients:

- 2 and ½ pounds of ground turkey
- 1 and ½ cups of chicken-flavor stuffing mix
- 2 large bean eggs
- ⅓ Cup of milk

Instructions:

1. Preheat your oven to a temperature of 350 degrees F (175 degrees C).
2. Mix all together with the turkey, the stuffing, eggs, and the milk in a large bowl.
3. Spread the mixture in a loaf pan of about 9x5 inches
4. Bake for about 1 hour until the temperature reads about 165 degrees F in the middle of the loaf

5. Serve and enjoy your dish!

Nutrition Information

Calories: 222.3, Fat: 9.5g, Carbohydrates: 13g, Dietary Fiber: 0.8g, Protein: 20.2g

Recipe 15: Baked Duck

(Prep time: 10 Minutes|Cook Time: 45 minutes| Servings: 5-6)

Ingredients:

- 1 Frozen duck of about 4 pounds frozen
- 6 Tablespoons of olive oil
- 2 Cups of dry sherry
- 3 teaspoons of dried oregano
- 3 teaspoons of dried rosemary
- 3 teaspoons of dried basil

Instructions:

1. Thaw the duck in the refrigerator until it is partially thawed. The inside should be frozen and the skin should be soft

2. Remove the duck out of the wrapping; then stab the duck about 15 to 20 times and make sure the holes go past the fat and right into the meat

3. In a large bowl; combine 1 cup of sherry with 3tablespoons of olive oil; then place the duck in a mixing bowl and spread the sherry and the olive oil over the duck; then cover the mixing bowl and let refrigerate until the duck is thawed

4. Preheat your oven to a temperature of about 375°F

5. Remove the duck from the marinade; then remove the giblets and the neck bone from the inside of the duck

6. Spread some of the prepared marinades in the duck; then rub the outside of the duck with about 3 tablespoons of olive oil with the basil, the rosemary, and the oregano

7. Pour the remaining cup of sherry into the bottom of a roasting pan; then place the duck in a pan

8. Roast for about 28 to 30 minutes per ½ pound and baste every about 30 to 45 minutes.

9. Remove the duck from the oven and set aside to cool for about 7 minutes

10. Serve and enjoy your dish!

Nutrition Information

Calories: 346, Fat: 21.8g, Carbohydrates: 13.4g, Dietary Fiber: 0.7g, Protein: 17.2g

Recipe 16: Fruit Stuffed Pork Loin

(Prep time: 10 Minutes|Cook Time: 45 minutes| Servings: 5-6)

Ingredients:

- ¾ cup of chopped pitted prunes
- ¾ cup of chopped dried apricots
- 1 tablespoon of grated fresh ginger
- 1 teaspoon of grated orange zest
- ½ teaspoon of ground cumin
- ½ teaspoon of ground cinnamon
- 1 pinch of salt and 1 pinch of ground black pepper to taste
- 1 Butterflied boneless pork loin roast; (4 pounds)

- ¼ Cup of packed brown sugar
- 2 teaspoons of all-purpose flour
- 2 teaspoons of cider vinegar
- 1 teaspoon of ground cumin
- 1 teaspoon of mustard powder
- ½ cup of water
- 1 teaspoon of cornstarch
- 1 tablespoon of water

Instructions:

1. Preheat your oven to a temperature of about 325 degrees F (165 degrees C).

2. Mix the prunes with the apricots, the ginger, the orange zest, about ½ teaspoon of cumin, and the cinnamon in a large bowl; then season with the salt and the black pepper.

3. Open the pork roast and spoon the stuffing into the center; then fold the meat over the stuffing and tie very well in a few places with kitchen twine; then set the roast over a rack in a large roasting pan

4. Combine the brown sugar, the flour, the cider vinegar, about 1 teaspoon of cumin, and the mustard powder into a paste; then spread the brown sugar mixture over the roast.

5. Bake in a preheated oven for about 1 and ½ hours

6. Transfer the roast to a serving platter and tent the meat with an aluminum foil

7. Skim the fat from the roasting pan and transfer the defatted drippings to a small saucepan.

8. Pour in ½ cup of water into the roasting pan and scrape up; then dissolve any browned bits of food into the water; pour into the saucepan with the pan juices.

9. Bring the pan juices to a boil over medium heat; then dissolve the cornstarch in 1 tablespoon of water in a small bowl and whisk into the pan juices and stir for about 1 minute

10. Strain the gravy into a gravy boat; then serve and enjoy your dish!

Nutrition Information

Calories: 435.4, Fat: 20.1g, Carbohydrates: 25.4g, Dietary Fiber: 2.2g, Protein: 37.5g

Recipe 17: Chicken with carrots and dates

(Prep time: 30 Minutes|Cook Time: 45 minutes| Servings: 5)

Ingredients:

- 1 teaspoon of lemon zest
- 3 tablespoons of freshly squeezed lemon juice, from 1 large lemon
- 1 teaspoon of orange zest
- 6 tablespoons of freshly squeezed orange juice, from 2 oranges
- 6 tablespoons of extra-virgin olive oil
- 3 Tablespoons of whole grain mustard
- 6 tablespoons of honey
- ½ teaspoon of crushed red pepper flakes
- 3 roughly chopped garlic cloves garlic

- 1 tablespoon of fresh thyme leaves
- 2 and ½ teaspoons of salt
- 4 pounds of bone-in chicken pieces (breasts, thighs, and drumsticks)
- 3 cups of ¼-inch sliced carrots
- 1 medium halved and thinly sliced yellow onion
- 1 cup of thinly sliced dried dates
- 2 tablespoons of chopped Italian parsley, for garnishing
- 2 light and dark parts of scallions, thinly sliced
- ¼ cup of chopped salted pistachios

Instructions:

1. Start by making the marinade and to do that; whisk all together with the lemon juice with the lemon zest, the orange juice, the olive oil, the mustard, the honey, the red pepper flakes, the garlic, the thyme, and the salt.

2. Put the chicken, the carrots the onions and the dates in a large plastic bag; then add the marinade and seal the bag

3. Massage your ingredients to make sure everything is evenly coated with the marinade

4. Put the bag over a rimmed sheet pan to protect against any leakage and marinate in the refrigerator for about 6 hours

5. Preheat your oven to a temperature of 425°F and place an oven rack in the middle position of the oven

6. Transfer all your ingredients from the bag to a rimmed sheet pan; then turn the chicken side up and roast for about 40 to 45 minutes

7. Stir the carrots half the way through

8. Turn on the broiler and cook for about 1 to 3 additional minutes

9. Transfer the chicken, the carrots, the onions, and the dates to a serving platter with the sauce in the pan and sprinkle with the parsley; the scallions and the pistachios

10. Top with the nuts; then serve and enjoy your dish!

Nutrition Information
Calories: 403, Fat: 23g, Carbohydrates: 19g, Dietary Fiber: 3g, Protein: 30g

Recipe 18: Beef Brisket with onion

(Prep time: 30 Minutes|Cook Time: 45 minutes| Servings: 5)

Ingredients:

- 1 Beef chuck roast of about 2,2 lbs with the bone
- 2 tbsp of olive oil
- 3 Finely chopped onions
- 2 Finely chopped garlic cloves
- 1 Cup of 250 ml of beef or chicken broth
- 6 medium peeled and cut carrots, into chunks
- 1 Pinch of salt
- 1 Pinch of pepper

Instructions:

1. Preheat your oven to a temperature of about 165 °C (325 °F).

2. In a large heavy skillet, sauté the meat on both the sides into the hot oil

3. Season with the salt and the pepper; then add in the garlic and sauté for about 1 minute

4. Deglaze your skillet with the broth and let boil over the roast

5. Put the carrots around your roast and cover with an aluminum foil

6. Roast for about 3 hours

7. Serve and enjoy with mashed potatoes and rice!

Nutrition Information

Calories: 212.6, Fat: 8.1g, Carbohydrates: 6.9g, Dietary Fiber: 0.9g, Protein: 27.2g

Recipe 19: Chicken with Olives and nuts

(Prep time: 6 Minutes|Cook Time: 15 minutes| Servings: 4)

Ingredients:

- 6 to 7 boneless chicken breast halves
- 5 to 6 Pitted and cut into pieces Medjool dates
- 2/3 Cup of red wine vinegar
- 2 tablespoons of olive oil
- ¾ cup of toasted California walnut pieces
- 1/3 cup of nicoise or pitted and sliced kalamata olives
- 3/4 cup of concentrated chicken stock

Instructions:

1. Combine vinegar with the dates in a small bowl and set aside for about an hour
2. Preheat your oven to a temperature of 325°F.

3. Heat the oil in a large heavy ovenproof skillet over medium-high heat; then add in the chicken and sauté for about 12 to 14 minutes or until it is fully cooked; then transfer the chicken to a serving platter; you can place over a bed of polenta

4. Put the skillet over high heat; then add in the walnuts, the olives, and the stock together with the dates and the vinegar

5. Boil rapidly for a moment; then scrape the bottom of the pan with a spatula to remove any bits

6. Add in the butter and the parsley and stir until the butter starts melting; then season with salt and pepper

7. Garnish with the onion walnut and the pancetta topping

8. Pour over the chicken; then serve and enjoy your dish!

Nutrition Information

Calories: 403, Fat: 23g, Carbohydrates: 19g, Dietary Fiber: 3g, Protein: 30g

Recipe 20: Smoked salmon rolls with cream cheese

(Prep time: 10 Minutes|Cook Time: 0 minutes| Servings: 3)

Ingredients:

- 4 to 5 slices of smoked salmon
- ½ Apple
- ½ Cup of cream cheese
- 2 tablespoons of liquid cream
- 2 to 3 sprigs of chives
- 2 to 3 sprigs of dill
- A few black sesame seeds
- 1 pinch of pepper

Instructions:

1. Mix the cream cheese in a bowl, then add the liquid cream, then the pepper to the mixture and chop it with the chives and mix very well
2. Peel the reserved apple, then remove the core and cut it into thin slices

3. Cut the smoked salmon into strips of about 10 cm of length
4. Arrange the thin apple slices on the salmon; then add a small amount of cream cheese mixture; then roll up all the ingredients
5. To finish the recipe, sprinkle black sesame on your dish and keep the dish fresh before serving it
6. Serve the recipe and enjoy it!

Nutrition Information

Calories: 90, Fat: 9g, Carbohydrates: 1g, Dietary Fiber: 0g, Protein: 3g

Recipe 21: Pork Pie

(Prep time: 10 Minutes|Cook Time: 35 minutes| Servings: 4)

Ingredients

- ½ Teaspoon of olive oil for the pan
- 2 Lightly beaten eggs
- 1 Pinch of salt
- ½ Teaspoon of garlic powder
- ½ teaspoon of onion powder
- ¼ Teaspoon of dried oregano
- 1/8 Teaspoon of cayenne pepper
- 1Tablespoon of Dijon Mustard
- 1 ½ Tablespoon of tomato paste
- ½ Tablespoon of lean ground pork
- ¼ Cups of shredded cheddar, divided

Instructions:

1. Preheat your oven to a temperature of about 350° F.
2. Grease a pie plate of about 9 inches with olive oil; then place it over a foiled-lined baking sheet
3. In a large mixing bowl, whisk the eggs with the salt, the garlic powder, the onion powder, the dried oregano, and the cayenne

4. Whisk in the Dijon mustard and the tomato paste; then set the egg mixture aside.
5. Heat a large skillet over medium-high heat; then add the ground pork and cook the mixture for about 5 minutes
6. Drain the meat; then let cool for a few minutes
7. Combine the drained and cooked pork; then let it cool slightly.
8. Combine the cooked and drained ground beef into the mixture of the eggs; then add in 1 cup of shredded cheddar
9. Transfer the prepared mixture to the prepared pie plate and pack it in; then make sure to smooth the top and the sides out
10. Sprinkle the remaining quantity of cheddar cheese on top
11. Bake for about 30 minutes; then let it cool for about 15 minutes
12. Serve and enjoy!

Nutrition Information

Calories: 405, Fat: 27g, Carbohydrates: 5g, Dietary Fiber: 1g, Protein: 32g

Recipe 22: Pork Fajitas

(Prep time: 15 Minutes|Cook Time: 20 minutes| Servings: 5)

Ingredients

To prepare the marinade:
- 6 Minced garlic cloves
- ¼ Cup of extra virgin olive oil
- ¼ Cup of coconut aminos
- 1 and ½ teaspoons of cumin
- 1Teaspoon of chili powder
- ¼ Cup of chopped cilantro
- The Juice and the zest of two limes

To prepare the Fajitas

- 1 Pound of pork skirt steak
- 1 Pinch of sea salt
- 1 Pinch of black pepper
- 1 Sliced red bell pepper

- 1 Sliced yellow bell pepper
- 1 Sliced green bell pepper
- 1 Large, sliced onion
- 2 Stemmed and seeded jalapeños, stem and seeds removed, sliced into strips
- 2 Sliced avocados
- 1 Chopped tomato
- ¼ Cup of finely chopped cilantro

Instructions:

1. Combine all of your ingredients into a zip-top plastic bag of 1-gallon size.
2. Put the skirt steak into the prepared bag; then remove any excess of excess air; then seal the bag and shake it or massage it
3. Put the steak bag in the refrigerator and let marinate for about 60 minutes
4. Heat a non-stick iron pan over medium heat; then remove the steak from the refrigerator and the bah; then season both its sides with a pinch of salt and a little bit of black pepper
5. Put the steak over the pan; then sear it for about 5 minutes
6. Flip your steak; then cook it for 5 additional minutes
7. Remove the steak from the wok; then put it over a cutting board and cover it with a foil
8. Scrape any excess of fats and add the onion, the jalapeños, and the pepper.
9. Add your marinade; the same you used to sauté your meat to sauté the vegetables for about 5 minutes
10. Slice the steak and arrange it in a serving platter with the rest of your ingredients and veggies
11. Top your dish with the avocado slices, the chopped tomato, and the cilantro.
12. Serve and enjoy your dish!

Nutrition Information

Calories: 250.7, Fat: 17.3g, Carbohydrates: 1g, Dietary Fiber: 0.1g, Protein: 22.4g

Recipe 23: Pork with orange sauce

(Prep time: 15 Minutes|Cook Time: 15 minutes| Servings: 3)

Ingredients
- 1 Pound of pork sirloin steak
- 1 Tablespoon of coconut aminos
- 1/3 Cup of almond flour
- 2 Tablespoons of melted coconut oil

The ingredients for the sauce

- 1 Tablespoons of almond flour
- 1/3 Cup of fresh orange juice
- 3 Tablespoons of molasses
- 1 Tablespoon of rice vinegar
- 2 Minced garlic cloves
- ¼ Teaspoon of minced fresh ginger
- ¼ Cup of thinly sliced orange rind
- ¼ Cup of finely chopped green onion

Instructions:

1. Cut the meat into pieces of the same size
2. Add the coconut aminos to the pieces of meat pieces and toss the ingredients altogether.
3. Add in the almond flour and coat your meat pieces very well
4. Put a wire rack in a cookie tray; then spread the pieces of meat into 1 single layer and set it aside to rest for about 40 minutes
5. When you only have about 10 minutes left before removing the meat from the freezer; pour the oil into a large non-stick wok.
6. Let the oil heat for about 5 minutes
7. Prepare a bowl and line it with a paper towel; then start frying the meat and cook it until it becomes golden for around 3 minutes per side.
8. Line a bowl with a paper towel and start frying meat
9. Remove the pieces of meat to the paper towel; then keep frying the remaining quantity until all of your meat is done.
10. Now, time to prepare the sauce of orange by mixing about 2 tablespoons of the almond flour with 1/3 cup of fresh orange juice, 3 tablespoons of molasses, 1 tablespoon of rice vinegar, 3 minced garlic cloves, about 1 teaspoon of fresh ginger, ¼ cup of minced thinly sliced orange rind and ¼ cup of finely chopped green onion.
11. Combine all of your sauce ingredients into a small and deep saucepan, then whisk and let the sauce boil for about 2 to 3 minutes.
12. Serve and enjoy your dish!

Nutrition Information

Calories: 231.6, Fat: 10.2g, Carbohydrates: 1.5g, Dietary Fiber: 0.2g, Protein: 31.5g

Recipe 24: Pork with Chimichurri

(Prep time: 10 Minutes|Cook Time: 20 minutes| Servings: 3-4)

Ingredients:

- ½ Teaspoon of sea salt
- ½ Teaspoon of fresh cracked pepper
- ½ Teaspoon of Spanish paprika
- ⅛ Teaspoon of cayenne powder
- 2 Bone-in Pork chops.
- 1 Tablespoon of coconut oil
- 1 Cup of Broccolini
- 1 Teaspoon of olive oil
- Lemon wedges

To prepare the Chimichurri:

- 1 Tablespoon of fresh chopped parsley
- 1 Tablespoon of olive oil
- 1 Tablespoon of cider vinegar
- 2 Minced garlic cloves

- ¼ Teaspoon of oregano
- ¼ Teaspoon of chili flakes
- ¼ Teaspoon of sea salt
- 1 splash of water

Instructions:

1. Preheat a BBQ to medium-low heat.
2. In a small and deep bowl, combine altogether the fresh cracked pepper with the sea salt, the fresh cracked pepper, the paprika, and the optional cayenne.
3. Drizzle about ½ teaspoon of the olive oil over both sides of each of the pork chops
4. Put the pork chops over the BBQ; then bake it for about 15 minutes
5. Flip the pork chops over the other side and cook it for 5 additional minutes; put the Broccolini into a medium bowl and after that toss it with the sea salt; then cook for about 9 minutes
6. Meanwhile; prepare the sauce of chimichurri by blending all the ingredients in a blender for about 2 minutes
7. Serve the pork with the Broccolini and the lemon wedges as well as with the chili flakes right on top.
8. Enjoy your dish!

Nutrition Information

Calories: 485, Fat: 36g, Carbohydrates: 10g, Dietary Fiber: 3g, Protein: 31g

Recipe 25: Beef Teryaki

(Prep time: 6 Minutes|Cook Time: 35 minutes| Servings: 3-4)

Ingredients:

- 1 Pound of cubed lean beef
- 1 Can of 4 ounces of crushed pineapple in juice
- ¼ Cup of water
- 1 Tablespoon of coconut aminos
- ¼ Teaspoon of ground ginger
- ¼ Teaspoon of garlic powder
- 1 Tablespoon of almond flour
- Cooked Cauliflower rice

Instructions:

1. Place the pineapple with its juice in a large pot over a medium-high heat
2. Pour in the water, the coconut aminos and the spices to the pan
3. Stir your ingredients very well

4. Add in the beef and cover the pan
5. Cook on a low heat for about 25 minutes
6. Combine the almond flour with 2 tablespoons of warm water
7. Pour the mixture in a pan and cook for about 10 additional minutes
8. Serve and enjoy your dish with cauliflower rice!

Nutrition Information

Calories: 249, Fat: 14.5g, Carbohydrates: 10g, Dietary Fiber: 3g, Protein: 31g

Recipe 26: Chicken curry

(Prep time: 6 Minutes|Cook Time: 35 minutes| Servings: 3-4)

Ingredients:

- 1 Chicken breast
- 1 Cup of fat-free yogurt
- ½ Bowl of fresh grapes
- ½ Cup of pomegranate seeds
- ½ Cucumber, diced
- 1 Tablespoon of curry powder to taste
- 1 Pinch of salt to taste
- 2 Tablespoons of almonds
- 2 to 3 chopped lettuce leaves

Instructions:

1. Place the chicken slices in boiling water and allow it to poach for 20-30 minutes.
2. Meanwhile, place the yogurt in a bowl and add in the grapes, pomegranate, cucumber, salt, walnuts; curry powder and give it a good mix.
3. Use a fork to shred the pieces of chicken and add it to the salad and mix well.
4. Add chopped lettuce and serve your delicious dish!

Nutrition Information
Calories: 286, Fat: 14g, Carbohydrates: 12g, Dietary Fiber: 2g, Protein: 29g

Recipe 27: Ground beef and sweet potato skillet

(Prep time: 10 Minutes|Cook Time: 30 minutes| Servings: 4)

Ingredients:

- 1 lb of ground beef, ground
- ½ medium onion, finely diced
- 1 Medium green bell pepper, finely diced
- 1 Garlic clove, minced
- ¼ tsp paprika
- ¼ tsp cumin, ground
- ¼ Teaspoon of Chilli powder
- 1 tsp oregano, dried
- 1 TBSP coconut oil, melted
- 2 Medium green onions, sliced
- 1 Pinch sea salt
- 1 Pinch black pepper, freshly ground

- 1 Teaspoon of chili powder
- ¼ tsp cumin
- 1 Pinch salt
- 1 pinch black pepper; freshly ground

Instructions:

1. Preheat an oven to 425° F.
2. In a large bowl; combine the lime juice, olive oil, chili powder, lime juice, cumin, pepper and salt
3. Toss the potatoes into the mixture and coat well; then transfer the potatoes to a baking sheet
4. Place the baking sheet in the oven and roast the potatoes for 18 to 20 minutes
5. Melt the coconut oil in a large skillet over medium-high heat and add in the onion; then sauté for about 2 minutes
6. Add the garlic and sauté for about 1 additional minute
7. Add in the ground beef and cook for about 7 minutes; then add in the bell pepper and cook for about 3 minutes
8. Add the cumin, chili powder, oregano and paprika, and season with 1 pinch salt and pepper
9. Garnish with finely chopped green onions
10. Serve and enjoy your dish!

Nutrition Information

Calories: 284, Fat: 16g, Carbohydrates: 9g, Dietary Fiber: 2.1g, Protein: 25g

Recipe 28: Bacon-wrapped fillet mignon

(Prep time: 6 Minutes|Cook Time: 25 minutes| Servings: 3-4)

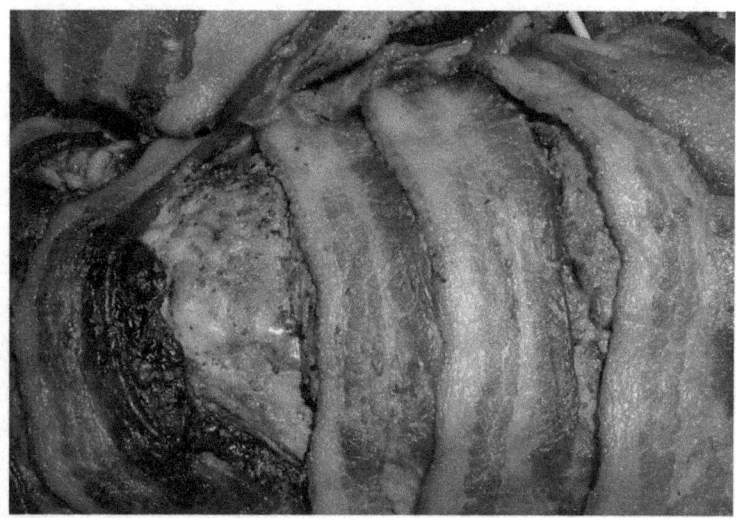

Ingredients:

- 2 Beef filet mignon
- 4 to 5 Pieces of bacon
- ⅛ Teaspoon of garlic powder
- 1 Pinch of salt
- 1 Pinch of black pepper
- 2 Tablespoons of mustard

Instructions:

1. Preheat your oven to about 375 degrees Fahrenheit
2. Wrap each of the beef filet mignons with the pieces of the bacon so that you cover all the parts of the sides of the beef filet mignon.
3. Secure the filets off the beef mignon with the help of toothpicks and sprinkle a little bit of garlic powder, a little bit of salt and 1 pinch of black pepper
4. Put a large saucepan over medium-high heat; then put each of the filets mignons and sauté it until it is perfectly cooked

5. Sear both of the tops and the bottoms of the fillets for about 3 minutes over each side
6. Transfer the mignon to the oven and add to it the mustard
7. Bake for about 7 to 8 minutes
8. Once cooked, serve and enjoy your dish!

Nutrition Information

Calories: 370, Fat: 22g, Carbohydrates: 2g, Dietary Fiber: 2.1g, Protein: 43g

Recipe 29: Salmon with orange juice

(Prep time: 5 Minutes|Cook Time: 10 minutes| Servings: 4)

Ingredients:

Ingredients for the salmon:

- 1 lb of salmon fillet
- 2 tsp of ghee
- 1 tsp ginger, ground
- 1 Pinch salt
- 1 pinch of black pepper, freshly ground

For the orange sauce:

- 1 TBSP of lemon, Juice
- 3 Tbsp of orange juice
- 1 Tbsp of coconut oil, melted

Instructions:

1. Melt the coconut oil in a heavy cast-iron skillet over a medium-high heat

2. Sprinkle the salmon with ginger, sea salt, and paprika
3. Make the orange sauce by stirring the juiced lemon with the orange juice and the melted coconut oil in a jar and shake the mixture
4. Place the salmon in the skillet and with the skin side down and cook for about 4 minutes
5. Lower the heat and flip the salmon to cook for about 4 minutes
6. Remove the salmon from the skillet and let rest for 2 minutes
7. Place the cooked salmon on a serving platter and serve it with the orange sauce
8. Enjoy your dish!

Nutrition Information
Calories: 339, Fat: 14g, Carbohydrates: 9.9g, Dietary Fiber: 0.7g, Protein: 13.5g

Recipe 30: Baked Barramundi with olives

(Prep time: 6 Minutes|Cook Time: 12 minutes| Servings: 3-4)

Ingredients:

- 2 Fillets of Barramundi, of about 5 to 6 oz each
- 2 Teaspoons of olive oil
- 2 Teaspoons of Szeged Fish Rub, for rubbing the fish
- ¼ Cup of finely chopped cherry tomatoes
- ¼ Cup of finely chopped black olives
- ¼ Cup of finely chopped green olives
- 1 Tablespoon of lemon zest
- 1 Tablespoons of freshly-squeezed lemon juice
- 2 Tablespoons of finely chopped fresh parsley
- 1 Tablespoon of olive oil
- 1 Pinch of salt
- 1 Pinch of fresh ground black pepper

Instructions

1. Let the fish thaw for an overnight or during all the day in the refrigerator

2. If the fillets have a thin fish on the side; you should trim it
3. Turn on your oven to a temperature of about 400° F to preheat it
4. Rub both the sides of the fish with the olive oil and sprinkle with the fish rub
5. Place the fish over a roasting sheet; then let the fish come to the room temperature while your oven starts heating
6. Chop the cherry tomatoes, the black olives, and the green olives; then zest the lemon and then squeeze its juice
7. Measure 2 tablespoons of lemon juice; then chop 2 tablespoons of flat or curly parsley
8. Stir all together with the black olives with the green olives, the lemon zest, the lemon juice, and the oil and mix very well
9. Season with 1 pinch of salt and 1 pinch of pepper
10. Place the fish in the oven and roast for about 10 to 12 minutes
11. Serve and enjoy your dish!

Nutrition Information

Calories: 339, Fat: 14g, Carbohydrates: 9.9g, Dietary Fiber: 0.7g, Protein: 13.5g

CHAPTER 4: Soups & Salads (~10 recipes)

Recipe 31: Chicken and Cheese Soup

(Prep time: 5 Minutes|Cook Time: 20 minutes| Servings: 4)

Ingredients:

- 1 ½ Large poblano peppers
- 2 Tablespoons of coconut oil, melted
- ½ medium yellow onion, chopped
- 4 Oz of riced cauliflower
- 2 Minced garlic cloves
- 1 ½ Cups of Chicken Broth
- 3 Ounces of cream cheese softened
- ¼ Teaspoon of seasoned salt
- 1 Pinch of black pepper, to taste
- ½ lb of cooked and shredded chicken
- ½ Cup of shredded cheddar cheese

Instructions

1. Heat the broiler on the oven and place the oven rack close to the top.

2. Remove the top of the poblano peppers; then scoop out the seeds and slice into half.
3. Place the poblano peppers on a cookie sheet and roast for about 2 minutes per side or until the skin is blackened
4. Remove from the oven and transfer the peppers to a ziplock bag; then let the peppers cool.
5. Once the peppers become cool to the touch, peel off the outer layer of the skin; then chop the peppers and set it aside.
6. In a heavy pot, melt the coconut oil over medium-high heat; then add the onion, the cauliflower, and the garlic and cook for about 5 to 7 minutes
7. Add the cream cheese and stir until the cream cheese is perfectly melted.
8. Add in the chopped peppers and slowly pour in the broth and stir
9. Add the seasoned salt and the pepper
10. With an immersion blender, puree your ingredients very well
11. Add the chicken and let simmer for about 10 minutes; then add the cheddar cheese and stir
12. Serve and enjoy your soup!

Nutrition Information

Calories: 209, Fat: 16g, Carbohydrates: 9g, Dietary Fiber: 2g, Protein: 10g

Recipe 32: Broccoli Soup

(Prep time: 8 Minutes|Cook Time: 25 minutes| Servings: 3)

Ingredients:

- ½ Cup of coconut oil, melted
- ¼ Yellow onion, chopped
- 1 Finely minced garlic clove
- 1/8 Cup of almond flour
- ½ Cup of low sodium chicken stock
- ½ Cup of half and half
- 1 Pinch of salt
- 1 Pinch of black pepper
- ¼ Teaspoon of vegetable stock powder
- ¼ Teaspoon of mustard powder
- ¼ Teaspoon of garlic powder
- ¼ Pound of chopped broccoli florets
- ½ Peeled and grated large carrots
- ½ Cups of low-fat sharp cheddar cheese

Instructions:

1. Melt the coconut oil in a large pot or a Dutch oven over medium heat.
2. Sauté the onion for about 2 minutes; then add in the garlic and cook for 1 additional minute
3. Whisk in the flour and cook for several minutes
4. Reduce the heat to low and slowly pour in the chicken stock and the half and half while stirring very well
5. Season with 1 pinch of salt and 1 pinch of pepper, then add in the stock powder, the mustard powder, and the garlic powder and give the mixture a good stir
6. Add in the carrots and the broccoli and let simmer for about 20 additional minutes
7. Mix in the cheese and stir; then season with salt and pepper
8. Serve and enjoy your soup!

Nutrition Information

Calories: 150, Fat: 7g, Carbohydrates: 15g, Dietary Fiber: 1g, Protein: 5g

Recipe 33: Green Asparagus Soup

(Prep time: 5 Minutes|Cook Time: 6 minutes| Servings: 3-4)

Ingredients:

- ½ Tablespoon of avocado oil
- 4 Ounces of trimmed and chopped fresh asparagus
- 1 Pinch of salt
- 1 Pinch of pepper
- ¼ Chopped green onion
- 1 Minced garlic clove
- 1 Cup of chicken broth
- ½ Ounce of fresh baby spinach
- ½ Cup of coconut cream
- ½ Tablespoon of fresh lemon juice

Instructions:

1. In a medium saucepan and over medium heat, heat the oil until it starts shimmering.
2. Add in the asparagus and sprinkle with 1 pinch of salt and 1 pinch of pepper; then sauté until it becomes bright green for about 3 to 4 minutes.
3. Add in the green onion and the garlic and cook for about 1 minute
4. Add in the broth and bring to a boil; then reduce the heat to a simmer and cook for about 10 to 12 minutes
5. Add in the spinach and cook for about 2 minutes; then transfer to a blender or a food processor and return the soup to the pan
6. Add in the coconut cream and the lemon juice it is very well combined; then adjust the seasoning
7. Serve and enjoy your soup!

Nutrition Information

Calories: 311, Fat: 28g, Carbohydrates: 6g, Dietary Fiber: 1.1g, Protein: 5g

Recipe 34: Mushroom Soup

(Prep time: 5 Minutes|Cook Time: 10 minutes| Servings: 3)

Ingredients:

- 2 Tablespoons of almond butter
- ½ Tablespoon of chopped fresh sage
- 1/3 lb of sliced mushrooms
- 1.33 cups of vegetable or chicken broth
- 1 Pinch of salt
- 1 Pinch of pepper
- 0.17 Cup of heavy cream

Instructions

1. In a large pot and over medium-high heat, melt the almond butter over medium-high heat for about 3 minutes
2. Add in the sage and cook for about 1 minute
3. Add in the mushrooms and stir to coat very well; then sauté until the mushrooms are perfectly tender and lightly browned for about 4 to 5 minutes.

4. Stir in the stock and bring the mixture to a simmer; then cook for about 4 to 5 additional minutes
5. Transfer your ingredients to a food processor or a blender
6. Process your ingredients until they become smooth
7. Return to the pot and stir in the cream
8. Serve and enjoy your soup!

Nutrition Information

Calories: 77, Fat: 3.4g, Carbohydrates: 3.4g, Dietary Fiber: 0.5g, Protein: 3.4g

Recipe 35: Carrot Soup

(Prep time: 5 Minutes|Cook Time: 35 minutes| Servings: 3-4)

Ingredients:

- 1 Cup of a chopped large onion
- ½ Pound of chopped carrots
- 5 Stalks of chopped celery
- 5 Cups of chopped kale
- 2 Tablespoons of coconut oil
- 2 Tablespoons of minced garlic
- 9 Cups of vegetable stock
- 1 Teaspoon of dried thyme
- 2 Bay leaves
- ¼ Teaspoon of dried rosemary
- ½ Teaspoon of coarse sea salt
- 1 Pinch of ground black pepper

Instructions:

1. Start by heating the coconut oil into a large saucepan, and when the oil I smelted; add in the onions and the garlic

2. Stir your ingredients very well and cook for about 3 minutes
3. Add the carrots and stir very well with the garlic and the onion; then let cook for about 5 minutes
4. Add the celery, the kale, the salt, the pepper, the rosemary, and the thyme.
5. Stir your ingredients very well and cook it for about 5 minutes
6. Add the vegetable stock and the bay leaves
7. Let your soup cook for about 30 minutes
8. Once your soup is ready; serve and enjoy its delicious taste.

Nutrition Information

Calories: 274, Fat: 15g, Carbohydrates: 8g, Dietary Fiber: 2g, Protein: 26g

Recipe 36: Tomato Soup

(Prep time: 5 Minutes|Cook Time: 35 minutes| Servings: 4)

Ingredients:

- 1 Medium, chopped onion
- 2 Teaspoons of minced garlic
- 1 Can of diced tomatoes
- 1 Teaspoon of dried oregano
- 1 Teaspoon of dried basil
- 1 Teaspoon of apple cider vinegar
- 1 Cup of vegetable broth
- ½ Cup of almond milk
- 1 Pinch of salt
- 1 Pinch of pepper

Instructions:

1. Heat a non-stick, large greased skillet over medium-high heat; then add the onion and let cook for about 5 minutes
2. Add in the garlic and let cook for about 1 minute

3. Toss in the tomatoes, the oregano, the basil, and the apple cider vinegar; then let boil
4. Once the soup starts boiling; add the almond milk and the broth; then let boil for about 20 minutes
5. Once your soup is ready, remove it from the heat and let it cool for 5 minutes; then puree it with an immersion blender
6. Serve and enjoy your tomato soup!

Nutrition Information

Calories: 159, Fat: 13g, Carbohydrates: 7g, Dietary Fiber: 3g, Protein: 4g

Recipe 37: Coconut Celery Soup

(Prep time: 6 Minutes|Cook Time: 30 minutes| Servings: 3)

Ingredients:

- 2 Tablespoons of coconut oil
- 1 Medium onion
- 1 Medium head of celery
- 1 and ½ cups of vegetable stock
- 1 Pinch of salt
- 1 Pinch of pepper
- 1 and ½ cups of coconut milk

Instructions:

1. Chop the celery and the onion
2. Heat the coconut oil into a saucepan; then pour in the stock

3. Let your ingredients simmer for about 25 minutes and make sure to stir from time to time
4. Once your soup is ready; let it cool for about 5 minutes; then let it simmer and puree it with an immersion blender
5. Pour the soup into bowls; then top it with parsley
6. Serve and enjoy your soup!

Nutrition Information

Calories: 227, Fat: 16g, Carbohydrates: 3g, Dietary Fiber: 2.7g, Protein: 18g

Recipe 38: Beets Salad

(Prep time: 5 Minutes|Cook Time: 5 minutes| Servings: 3)

Ingredients:

- 3 Cups of Mache
- 1 Julienned medium cooked beets
- ½ Sliced Cucumber
- 1 Cup of chopped broccoli
- ½ Shredded carrot
- ½ Julienned, Bell pepper
- 1 Tablespoon of chopped almonds

Ingredients to make the Almond Vinaigrette

- 1 Tablespoon of almond butter
- ¼ Tablespoon of olive oil
- ½ Tablespoon of freshly squeezed lemon juice
- ½ Tablespoon of maple syrup
- ½ Minced garlic clove
- 1 Tablespoon of white wine vinegar

- 1 Pinch of sea salt
- 1 Pinch of freshly ground black pepper

Instructions:

1. Into a deep bowl, combine your ingredients to make the almond vinaigrette; then whisk very well until your ingredients are very well mixed
2. Assemble your salad by mixing the ingredients altogether very well, except for the almonds
3. Drizzle your vinaigrette over your salad and toss the ingredients very well.
4. Top your salad with the chopped almonds
5. Serve and enjoy your salad!

Nutrition Information

Calories: 49, Fat: 3.2g, Carbohydrates: 3.3g, Dietary Fiber: 0.7g, Protein: 3g

Recipe 39: Cabbage Salad

(Prep time: 5 Minutes|Cook Time: 0 minutes| Servings: 3)

Ingredients:

- 1 Cup of shredded green cabbage
- ½ Cup of shredded red cabbage
- 2 Cups of shredded raw kale
- 2 Shredded carrots
- 1 Cored, peeled and thinly sliced apple
- ¼ Cup of slivered almonds
- ¼ Cup of fresh blueberries
- ¼ Cup of extra virgin olive oil
- 2 Tablespoons of apple cider vinegar
- 2 Tablespoons of swerve sweetener
- 1 Tablespoon of lemon juice
- 1 Pinch of sea salt
- 1 Pinch of freshly ground black pepper

Instructions:

1. In a deep salad bowl, combine the green cabbage with the red cabbage, the carrots, the kale, the apple, and the blueberries.
2. Into a small bowl, mix the olive oil, the apple cider vinegar, the swerve sweetener
3. Add the lemon juice; the salt and the pepper
4. Drizzle your vinaigrette over the salad and toss very well until your ingredients are very well blended
5. Top your salad with slivered almonds
6. Serve and enjoy your salad!

Nutrition Information

Calories: 70, Fat: 3.5g, Carbohydrates: 9g, Dietary Fiber: 3g, Protein: 3g

Recipe 40: Cesar Salad

(Prep time: 5 Minutes|Cook Time: 20 minutes| Servings: 2-3)

Ingredients:

- ¾ lb of chicken breasts
- 1 Tablespoon of olive oil
- 1 Pinch of salt and 1 pinch of pepper
- 3 Oz of bacon
- 5 Oz of Romaine lettuce
- 1 Oz of freshly grated parmesan cheese
- For the dressing
- ½ Cup of mayonnaise
- 1 Tablespoon of Dijon mustard
- ½ Lemon, both the zest and the juice
- ½ Oz of finely grated parmesan cheese
- 2 Tablespoons of finely chopped filets of anchovies
- 1 Finely chopped garlic clove
- 1 Pinch of salt
- 1 Pinch of pepper

Instructions

1. Preheat your to a temperature of about 350°F
2. Combine your ingredients of the dressing with an immersion blender and set aside in the refrigerator
3. Put the chicken breasts in a greased baking dish
4. Season the chicken with 1 pinch of salt and 1 pinch of pepper and drizzle the olive oil on top
5. Bake the chicken in an oven for about 20 minutes; then fry the bacon until it becomes crispy; then chop the lettuce and place it into the base onto two plates
6. Place the chicken in a serving platter and dress with grated cheese
7. Serve and enjoy your salad!

Nutrition Information

Calories: 90, Fat: 3.5g, Carbohydrates: 9g, Dietary Fiber: 3g, Protein: 3g

Snacks/Sides (~20 recipes)

Recipe 41: Sweet Potato Chips

(Prep time: 5 Minutes|Cook Time: 20 minutes| Servings: 3)

Ingredients:

- 2 Medium sweet potatoes
- 2 Tablespoons of coconut oil
- 2 Thickly cut garlic cloves
- ¼ Teaspoon of sea salt

Instructions:

1. Preheat your oven to a temperature of about 395° F.
2. Grease a large baking tray with a little quantity of coconut oil
3. Top the slices of the sweet potatoes with coconut oil
4. Place the potato chips into a baking tray and bake it for about 15 minutes
5. Remove the baking tray from the oven
6. Insert 1 piece of garlic into each of the sweet potato rounds
7. Sprinkle a pinch of salt and a pinch of pepper over the potatoes and bake it into the oven for about 5 minutes
8. Remove the tray from the oven

9. Serve and enjoy your fried sweet potatoes!

Nutrition Information

Calories: 92, Fat: 0.2g, Carbohydrates: 12.4g, Dietary Fiber: 2g, Protein: 2g

Recipe 42: Cheddar Cheese Crackers

(Prep time: 5 Minutes|Cook Time: 5 minutes| Servings: 3-4)

Ingredients:

- 4 Quartered slices of cheddar cheese
- A dip of your choice, like guacamole

Instructions:

1. On a parchment-lined baking sheet, place the quartered slices of cheese
2. Make sure to leave about 1 inch apart from each other on the baking sheet
3. Broil on high heat for about 3 to 5 minutes
4. Remove from the oven; then blot with a clean paper towel to remove any excess of oil
5. Serve and enjoy your snack!

Nutrition Information

Calories: 47, Fat: 4g, Carbohydrates: 0.4g, Dietary Fiber: 0.1g, Protein: 4g

Recipe 43: Parsnip Chips

(Prep time: 5 Minutes|Cook Time: 10 minutes| Servings: 4)

Ingredients:

- 2 parsnips
- 2 Tablespoons of coconut oil
- 1 Pinch of salt
- 1 Pinch of pepper

Instructions

1. Cut both the bottom and the top of the parsnip
2. With the help of a vegetable peeler, shred each of the parsnips into strips
3. Heat a generous quantity of coconut oil into a frying pan
4. Fry the parsnips until it becomes crispy
5. Season with 1 pinch of salt and 1 pinch of pepper

6. Serve and enjoy your snack!

Nutrition Information

Calories: 150, Fat: 12g, Carbohydrates: 9g, Dietary Fiber: 2g, Protein: 1g

Recipe 44: Avocado Hummus

(Prep time: 5 Minutes|Cook Time: 0 minutes| Servings: 3)

Ingredients:

- 1 Cup of unsalted macadamia nuts
- 1 Large avocado
- 1 Garlic clove
- 1 Tablespoon of tahini paste
- ½ Teaspoon of sea salt
- 2 Tablespoons of fresh lime juice
- 2 Tablespoons of extra virgin olive oil
- Chopped fresh cilantro

Instructions:

1. Start by placing the macadamia nuts in a container; then fill it with water
2. Let soak at the room temperature for about 2 hours or an overnight
3. Strain and rinse the macadamia nuts after soaking; hen discarding the liquid
4. Peel the avocado; then remove the seed; then peel the garlic and slice it
5. Add chopped fresh cilantro

6. Put your ingredients in a food processor; then process until your ingredients become smooth
7. Transfer to a bowl; then drizzle the olive oil on top and garnish with cilantro leaves
8. Serve with freshly chopped vegetables like carrots, celery sticks, and peppers!

Nutrition Information

Calories: 152, Fat: 12.4g, Carbohydrates: 9.5g, Dietary Fiber: 3.2g, Protein: 3.4g

Recipe 45: Crispy Roasted Kale

(Prep time: 5 Minutes|Cook Time: 9 minutes| Servings: 4)

Ingredients:

- 2 Large stalks kale, of about 4 cups of leaves
- 1 Tablespoon of avocado oil
- 1 and ½ tablespoons of nutritional yeast
- ½ Teaspoon of garlic powder
- ¼ Teaspoon of cumin
- ¼ Teaspoon of chili powder
- 1/8 Teaspoon of cayenne
- ¼ Teaspoon of pink salt

Instructions:

1. Preheat your oven to a temperature of about 300°F; then grease a large baking sheet and set it aside
2. Remove the leaves from the stalks of the kale; then cut the kale into large pieces
3. Wash the kale and dry it in a salad spinner; then make sure the kale is dry

4. You can also pat down the kale with a paper towel and let dry on a cooling rack
5. Place the dried kale leaves into a bowl; then drizzle on top about ½ tablespoon of avocado oil on the kale leaves
6. Massage the oil into the kale leaves; then sprinkle on about 1 tablespoon of nutritional yeast and the seasonings
7. Add in ½ tablespoon of oil and repeat the same process with your oiled hands and massage the yeast into the kale leaves
8. Transfer to a baking sheet; then arrange in one layer; then sprinkle on the rest of the yeast and add a pinch of salt
9. Bake the kale at a temperature of about 300° F for about 7 to 9 minutes
10. Let the kale cool for about 5 minutes; then serve and enjoy!

Nutrition Information

Calories: 135, Fat: 7.9g, Carbohydrates: 9.4g, Dietary Fiber: 0.5g, Protein: 8.7g

Recipe 46: Mashed broccoli

(Prep time: 5 Minutes|Cook Time: 5 minutes| Servings: 3-4)

Ingredients:

- ½ Pound of Broccoli
- ¼ Teaspoon of salt
- 1 Pinch of pepper
- 1 Ounce of Butter
- 1Ounce of Sour Cream
- ½ Tablespoon of finely chopped chives

Instructions:

1. Bring a large pot of water to a boil.
1. Chop the broccoli into florets of even size
2. Add in the broccoli to the boiling water and cook for about 3 to 5 minutes
3. Drain the broccoli and return it to the pot; then add in the butter, the cream, the salt, and the pepper
4. Blend the broccoli with a blender
5. Add in the chives and adjust the seasoning of salt and pepper
6. Serve and enjoy!

Nutrition Information

Calories: 59, Fat: 5g, Carbohydrates: 1g, Dietary Fiber: 1g, Protein: 4g

Recipe 47: Roasted Radish

(Prep time: 5 Minutes|Cook Time: 25 minutes| Servings: 4)

Ingredients:

- ½ lb of radishes with the ends trimmed and halved
- ½ Tablespoon of avocado oil
- ¼ Teaspoon of sea salt
- ¼ Teaspoon of pepper
- 2 to 3 tablespoons of finely minced garlic cloves
- ¼ Teaspoon of dried chives or parsley

Instructions:

1. Preheat your oven to a temperature of about 425°F.
2. In a large bowl, mix the radishes with the avocado oil, the salt, and the pepper and toss until the radishes are coated very well
3. Save the minced garlic to add it later
4. Spread the radishes out in a large baking dish; don't overcrowd your dish
5. Bake for about 20 to 25 minutes; then tossing every 10 minutes and add the garlic and the dried parsley and bake for about 5 additional minutes
6. Garnish with chopped parsley; then serve and enjoy your dish!

Nutrition Information

Calories: 91, Fat: 8g, Carbohydrates: 1g, Dietary Fiber: 1g, Protein: 4g

Recipe 48: Sweet Glazed Carrots

(Prep time: 5 Minutes|Cook Time: 25 minutes| Servings: 4)

Ingredients:

- 3 Medium carrots about ½ pounds
- 1 Tablespoon of extra virgin olive oil
- 1 Pinch of sea salt
- ¼ Teaspoon of freshly cracked black pepper
- 1Tablespoons of freshly chopped flat-leaf parsley for garnishing

For the carrot Low Carb Glaze:

- 2 Tablespoons of coconut oil, melted

Instructions:

1. Pre-heat your oven to a temperature of about 475° F degrees.
1. Wash and dry; then trim the carrots.

2. Cut the carrots both in a length-wise way; then into pieces of about 1 ½ inch each
3. In a large bowl; toss the carrots with the olive oil, the salt, and the pepper; then make sure to coat the carrots into the olive oil
4. Spread the carrots over a large cookie sheet; then place on the top rack of your oven
5. Roast for about 20 to 25 minutes
6. Cook the carrots until they become tender
7. Prepare the glaze in a skillet by melting the coconut oil and the swerve sweetener and mix with a wooden spoon
8. Let cook for about 4 to 5 minutes
9. Once the glaze is perfectly done; add in the sauce to the carrots and toss; then garnish with the finely chopped carrots
10. Serve and enjoy your delicious carrots!

Nutrition Information

Calories: 85, Fat: 7.4g, Carbohydrates: 3.9g, Dietary Fiber: 1g, Protein: 0.5g

Recipe 49: Baba Ghanoush

(Prep time: 6 Minutes|Cook Time: 10 minutes| Servings: 3-4)

Ingredients:

- ¼ lb of small zucchini of quartered lengthwise
- 1 ½ tbsp of olive oil, divided
- 1 Pinch of kosher salt
- 1 Pinch of black pepper
- 1 Garlic clove
- 1Tablespoons of tahini
- 1 Tablespoon of fresh lemon juice
- 1 Tablespoon of mint leaves
- 1 Tablespoon of pine nuts, toasted

Instructions:

1. Start by heating a grill to medium-high heat; then toss the zucchini with about 1 tablespoon of oil and 1 pinch of salt

2. Grill the zucchini for about 8 to 10 minutes; then transfer the zucchini to a blender with the garlic, the tahini, the lemon juice, and about 1 tablespoon of mint; then pulse to combine very well
3. Chop the remaining mint; then top with the mint and the pine nuts
4. Serve and enjoy your zucchini Baba Ghannoush
5. Enjoy!

Nutrition Information

Calories: 117, Fat: 8.7g, Carbohydrates: 3.9g, Dietary Fiber: 2.5g, Protein: 2.5g

Recipe 50: Red pepper Hummus

(Prep time: 5 Minutes|Cook Time: 5 minutes| Servings: 2-3)

Ingredients:

- 1 Halved and seeded red pepper
- ¼ lb of carrots
- 1 Finely minced garlic clove
- ¼ Cup of tahini
- 1 Tablespoon of fresh lemon juice
- ½ Teaspoon of smoked paprika
- ¼ Teaspoon of ground cumin
- 1 Pinch of Kosher salt
- 1 Pinch of pepper
- Chopped fresh dill, for sprinkling it

Instructions:

1. Peel the carrots and steam it or boil it into hot water

2. Heat a broiler; then place the pepper, with the cut sides down, over a rimmed baking sheet and broil for about charred, 4 to 5 minutes.
3. Transfer to a bowl; then cover, and let sit
4. Peel the peppers when it is cool enough to handle and discard the skin
5. Transfer the peppers and the carrots to a food processor
6. Add the garlic, the tahini, the lemon juice, the paprika, the cumin, and 1 pinch of salt with 1 pinch of pepper and puree the mixture until it becomes smooth
7. Sprinkle with dill; then serve and enjoy with vegetables!

Nutrition Information

Calories: 70, Fat: 6g, Carbohydrates: 3.9g, Dietary Fiber: 3g, Protein: 2g

Recipe 51: Stuffed Peppers

(Prep time: 10 Minutes|Cook Time: 8 minutes| Servings: 6)

Ingredients:

- 6 Large bell peppers, green or red
- ½ Pound of ground beef
- 1 Pinch of garlic salt
- 1 tsp basil, finely chopped
- ¼ tsp black pepper
- 1 Large egg, lightly beaten
- ¼ Cup coconut flour
- 1 TBSP olive oil

Instructions:

1. Start by cutting the tops off the bell peppers and remove the seeds; then set the peppers aside
2. In a large mixing bowl, combine the ground beef with the garlic salt, the egg, the coconut flour, the Italian seasoning, the basil, and the pepper

3. Stuffed the peppers with the mixture; then heat a large skillet over medium-high heat and spray it with olive oil
4. When the oil heats up, arrange the peppers and cook for about 5 minutes; then flip the pepper and cook it for about 3 additional minutes on the other side
5. Remove the stuffed peppers from the skillet and transfer it to a serving platter
6. Serve and enjoy your dish!

Nutrition Information

Calories: 243, Fat: 14g, Carbohydrates: 9g, Dietary Fiber: 2.9g, Protein: 21g

Recipe 52: Stuffed Mushrooms

(Prep time: 9 Minutes|Cook Time: 12 minutes| Servings: 6)

Ingredients:

To make the filling
- ¼ Medium, finely sliced brown onion
- ½ Teaspoon of olive oil
- 5 Finely chopped; sage leaves
- 1 Tablespoon of chopped almond flakes
- 1 Finely sliced garlic clove
- ½ Pound of grass-fed pork mince
- 1 Pinch of sea salt
- 1 Pinch of pepper

For the mushrooms
- 10 Button, cremini mushrooms
- 1 Tablespoon of balsamic vinegar
- 1 Tablespoons of virgin olive oil
- ½ Tablespoon of coconut aminos
- 1 Pinch of sea salt

To make the glaze:
- 1 Tablespoon of balsamic vinegar

- 1 Tablespoon of coconut aminos
- 1 Teaspoon of olive oil

Instructions:

1. Preheat your oven to a temperature of about 395 °F.
2. In a medium skillet; cook the onion into the olive oil for about 2 minutes over a medium heat
3. Add the sage leaves and the almonds; then cook for about 2 minutes
4. Transfer the ingredients you have cooked into a bowl with the raw beef mince
5. Add the garlic, the salt, and the pepper; then combine your ingredients very well
6. Assemble the meat with your hands; then remove the stumps of the mushroom heads
7. Mix the balsamic vinegar with the oil, the coconut aminos and the sea salt
8. With a pastry brush, rub the mushrooms with your marinade mixture; then fill each of the mushroom cavities with 1 tablespoon of the pork mixture
9. Arrange the mushrooms over a baking tray; then fill each of your mushrooms with 1 tablespoon of the pork mince
10. Line the stuffed mushrooms over a baking tray; then place it in the oven
11. Bake the mushrooms for about 20 minutes at a temperature of about 395° F; meanwhile, make the glaze by combining its ingredients into a medium skillet and let it simmer for about 15 minutes
12. Remove mushrooms from the oven and brush it with the balsamic glaze
13. Serve and enjoy your stuffed mushrooms!

Nutrition Information

Calories: 159, Fat: 12.3g, Carbohydrates: 9.3g, Dietary Fiber: 1.5g, Protein: 4.5g

Recipe 53: Pork Koftas

(Prep time: 11 Minutes|Cook Time: 7 minutes| Servings: 5-6)

Ingredients:

- 1 Large; English cucumber
- ½ Teaspoon of salt, divided
- 1 Medium lemon
- ½ Garlic cloves
- 1 Cup of plain Greek yogurt
- ½ Cup of fresh dill
- ½ Cup of fresh mint leaves
- 1 Tablespoon of extra-virgin olive oil
- ½ Teaspoon of freshly ground black pepper

Ingredients to make the Koftas:

- ½ Medium onion; yellow
- 1 Peeled ginger piece
- 2 Garlic cloves

- ¼ Cup of fresh parsley leaves
- ¼ Cup of fresh mint leaves
- 1 lb of grass-fed ground beef
- 1 Teaspoon of kosher salt
- 1 Tablespoon of ground cumin
- 1 Tablespoon of ground coriander
- ½ Teaspoon of ground cinnamon
- ½ Teaspoon of ground cloves
- 1 Pinch of red pepper flakes
- A little bit of olive oil

Instructions:

1. Start by making the salad: Peel the cucumber and grate it with a box grater; then put it into a bowl with about ½ teaspoon of salt; then set it aside for about 15 minutes
2. In the meantime; zest your lemons and make sure you have about 1 tablespoon of lemon zest
3. Transfer the lemon zest with the juice of a lemon to a medium bowl
4. Cut the dill and the mint; then add it to a bowl with the lemon zest
5. Add the oil, the yogurt, the pepper and about 1 teaspoon of salt; then mix very well
6. In a large bowl; grate your onion with a large hole of your box grater; then put ¼ cup into another bowl, also; grate the ginger and add 1 tablespoon of the grated ginger to the bowl with the onion
7. Grate the garlic and finely chop the parsley; then add the salt, the ground pork, and the spices; and mix it with your hands and combine very well
8. Form about 20 balls of about 2 inch the ball; then refrigerate it for about 30 minutes
9. Line the meatballs over a baking sheet; then heat a lightly greased grilling pan; then sauté the meatballs and grill it for about 6 minutes
10. Remove the meatballs to a serving dish and take the salad out of the refrigerator
11. Serve and enjoy your Pork Koftas!

Nutrition Information

Calories: 281, Fat: 20.1g, Carbohydrates: 5.4g, Dietary Fiber: 1.6g, Protein: 19.4g

Recipe 54: Stuffed Potatoes

(Prep time: 10 Minutes|Cook Time: 40 minutes| Servings: 7)

Ingredients:

- 3 Medium sweet potatoes
- 1 Tablespoon of coconut oil
- ½ Chopped small onion
- 1 Minced garlic cloves
- 1 Pound of grass-fed ground beef
- 1 Teaspoon of chili powder
- ¼ Teaspoon of cumin
- ¼ Teaspoon of sea salt
- 1 Cup of tomato sauce

Instructions:

1. Preheat your oven to a temperature of about 425°F
2. Scrub the sweet potatoes; then pierce its skin.
3. Put the sweet potatoes over a baking sheet; then bake for about 30 minutes

4. While your potatoes are being cooked; make the sauce by heating the coconut oil into a pan of a medium-size over a low heat
5. Add the onion and sauté it for about 4 minutes
6. Add the pork mince to your pan and sauté it for about 5 minutes
7. Add in the garlic and sauté for a few seconds
8. Add the cumin; the salt and the chili powder
9. Remove the sweet potatoes from the oven; then cut it open right into the middle
10. Stuff your potatoes with the filling of pork mince
11. Enjoy your dish!

Nutrition Information

Calories: 187, Fat: 5g, Carbohydrates: 15g, Dietary Fiber: 2g, Protein: 20g

Recipe 55: Beef Fritters

(Prep time: 6 Minutes|Cook Time: 8 minutes| Servings: 6-7)

Ingredients:

- ½ Pound of ground pork
- 2 Cooked bacon slices
- 4 Halved cherry tomatoes
- ½ Cup of chopped lettuce
- 2 Sliced pickles into
- 1 Pinch of sea salt
- 1 Pinch of freshly ground pepper

Instructions:

1. Preheat your grill to a medium-high heat
2. Season the meat with salt and pepper; then form patties
3. Arrange the patties over a grill; then cook it for about 3 minutes per side; then set it aside
4. Top each of your patties with 1 piece of bacon

5. Add 1 piece of pickle, tomato, and lettuce
6. Secure each of your patties simply, by using a toothpick
7. Serve and enjoy your beef fritters!

Nutrition Information

Calories: 301, Fat: 21g, Carbohydrates: 1g, Dietary Fiber: 2g, Protein: 26g

Recipe 56: Candied pork rinds

(Prep time: 5 Minutes|Cook Time: 10 minutes| Servings: 3-4)

Ingredients:

- A bag of 3.5 ounces of pork rinds
- ¼ Cup of melted coconut oil
- ¼ Cup of erythritol
- 1 Tablespoon of ground cinnamon

Instructions:

1. Place the pork rinds in a gallon Ziploc bag or large Tupperware.
2. Add the coconut oil; then shake the bag to coat the pork rinds very well
3. Sprinkle the cinnamon on top and add the erythritol and shake to coat
4. Serve and enjoy your dish!

Nutrition Information
Calories: 95, Fat: 6.2g, Carbohydrates: 2.8g, Dietary Fiber: 0.8g, Protein: 9.1g

Recipe 57: Stuffed Sardines

(Prep time: 10 Minutes|Cook Time: 12 minutes| Servings: 7)

Ingredients:

- 1 Avocado, with the seed, removed
- 1 Tin of sardines, drained
- 1 Tablespoon of low Carb mayonnaise
- 1 Medium spring onion or a bunch of chives
- 1 Tablespoon of fresh lemon juice
- ¼ Teaspoon of turmeric powder
- 1 Teaspoon of freshly ground turmeric root
- 1 Pinch of salt and 1 pinch of pepper, to taste

Instructions:

1. Slice the avocado and remove the seeds; then drain the sardines and place it in a bowl
2. Break into small pieces with a fork
3. Scoop the middle of the avocado out while leaving about ½ to 1 inch of the flesh of the avocado into the bowl with the sardines

4. Add in the finely sliced spring onion or the chives and the freshly grated Tumeric root
5. Add in the mayonnaise, then mix very well
6. Add the flesh of the scooped avocado and mash into the desired consistency; then squeeze in the fresh lemon juice and season with 1 pinch of salt.
7. Scoop the avocado mixture into each avocado half and enjoy it!

Nutrition Information

Calories: 242, Fat: 22g, Carbohydrates: 7g, Dietary Fiber: 4.9g, Protein: 6g

Recipe 58: Salmon Cakes

(Prep time: 5 Minutes|Cook Time: 5 minutes| Servings: 8)

Ingredients:

- 1 Pouch of 5 oz of pink salmon
- 1 Egg
- ¼ Cup of finely ground pork rinds
- ½ Finely chopped jalapeno
- 1 Tablespoon of Sarayo
- 1 Tablespoon of finely diced red onion
- ¼ Teaspoon of garlic powder
- ¼ Teaspoon of chili powder
- 1 Pinch of salt
- 1 Pinch of pepper
- ½ Tablespoon of avocado oil

Instructions:

1. In a large bowl; combine the salmon with the egg, the jalapeno, the Sarayo, the red onion, the ground pork rinds, and the seasoning
2. Form patties with the obtained mixture
3. In a large non- stick skillet, drizzle the oil and cook the patties over medium heat for about 4 to 5 minutes

4. Serve and enjoy your salmon cakes!

Nutrition Information

Calories: 281.5, Fat: 20.3g, Carbohydrates: 5.7g, Dietary Fiber: 2.1g, Protein: 20.5g

Recipe 59: Scotch Eggs

(Prep time: 7 Minutes|Cook Time: 19 minutes| Servings: 4)

Ingredients:

- ½ Pound of ground beef or ground chicken
- 1 Pinch of salt to taste
- 4 Hardboiled eggs

Instructions:

1. Preheat your oven to a temperature of about 350°F.
2. Line two baking sheets with parchment paper; then combine the ground beef with salt in a bowl
3. With both your hands; combine your ingredients and form small rimmed baking sheets with parchment paper
4. Combine the ground meat with the salt in a large bowl and form 4 meatballs
5. Place each meatball on each of the lined baking sheets and press it flat
6. Place one boiled eggs in the middle of each portion of flattened meat and wrap the meat around the egg making sure not to leave any holes or gaps
7. Bake for about 15 minutes; then turn them over, and cook for about 10 additional minutes
8. Place under the broiler for about 5 minutes
9. Serve and enjoy your scotch eggs!

Nutrition Information

Calories: 394.2, Fat: 26.8g, Carbohydrates: 3.9g, Dietary Fiber: 0.7g, Protein: 32.2g

Recipe 60: Spring Rolls

(Prep time: 10 Minutes|Cook Time: 20 minutes| Servings: 6)

Ingredients:

- 2 Tablespoons of ghee or olive oil
- 1 Peeled and grated medium carrot
- 1 Pinch of sea salt
- 1 Finely minced garlic clove
- 2 Large pasteurized eggs
- ¼ medium red onion, thinly sliced
- ¼ Small thinly sliced white onion
- 1 Pinch of freshly ground black pepper
- 1 Tablespoon of Coconut oil
- 1 Tablespoon of mayonnaise
- 1 Slice of free-range ham

Instructions:

1. Preheat the oven to a temperature of about 350 °F.
2. Heat the ghee in a medium heavy skillet; then add in the onion and sauté for about 4 minutes
3. Add in the grated carrot; then sprinkle with 1 pinch of salt and cook for about 5 minutes; make sure to stir from time to time to prevent burning and cook for 4 additional minutes
4. Add in the garlic with 1 pinch of salt and 1 pinch of pepper right by the end
5. Crack the eggs with 1 pinch salt in a bowl and whisk very well

6. Put a large parchment paper in an 8-9 by 14-15 oven tray and lightly spray with melted coconut oil or ghee
7. Pour in the egg batter and quickly tuck away the baking paper into its corners to make sure the batter won't escape from the corners
8. Pour the mixture of onion and carrots on top and spread it very well
9. Place the baking pan in the oven and bake for about 16 to 17 minutes
10. Remove the baking tray from the oven and carefully lift the baking paper
11. Place them over a cutting board and spread a little bit of mayonnaise and scattered ham
12. Without removing the baking paper, start rolling from the base and fold inwards the egg roll until you finish
13. Remove the paper off and slice the rolled egg; then serve and enjoy!

Nutrition Information

Calories: 110, Fat: 7g, Carbohydrates: 13g, Dietary Fiber: 1g, Protein: 4g

Dressings & Dips (~5 recipes)

Recipe 61: Spinach dip

(Prep time: 6 Minutes|Cook Time: 8 minutes| Servings: 3)

Ingredients:

- 1 ½ Cups of tightly packed, defrosted spinach
- 1 Tablespoon of coconut oil
- 1 Tablespoon of extra virgin olive oil
- 1 Small and thinly sliced brown onion
- ⅔ Teaspoon of sea salt
- 1 Finely diced, large garlic clove
- 1 A teaspoon of mild curry powder
- ¼ Cup of coconut cream
- 1 Tablespoon of lemon juice

Instructions:

1. Defrost the spinach; then put the frozen spinach balls or the blocks into a medium bowl with a little bit of hot water for about ½ an hour to 1 hour.
2. Strain; then squeeze any excess of liquid
3. Heat a medium frying pan over medium-high heat; then add the coconut oil let the ingredients simmer over low heat.
4. Add the salt and the onion; then sauté your ingredients for about 6 minutes and stir

5. Add the spinach; the garlic and the curry; the, stir for around 1 to minutes
6. Add the coconut cream with the lemon juice and stir very well for 1 additional minute until
7. Combine all of your ingredients; then season with the salt and pepper
8. Serve and enjoy your dip!

Nutrition Information

Calories: 45, Fat: 3.5g, Carbohydrates: 2g, Dietary Fiber: 0.1g, Protein: 0.5g

Recipe 62: Onion dip

(Prep time: 6 Minutes|Cook Time: 5 minutes| Servings: 3)

Ingredients:

- ½ Thinly sliced onion
- ½ Tablespoons of olive oil
- 1 Teaspoon of fresh thyme leaves
- 1 Pinch of kosher salt
- 1 Pinch of freshly ground pepper
- 1 Tablespoon of apple cider vinegar
- ½ Cup of Greek yogurt
- Crackers, for serving

Instructions:

1. Start by cooking the onions and to that heat the olive oil in a skillet over a medium-high heat

2. Add in the onion and the thyme and season with 1 pinch of salt and 1 pinch of pepper
3. Turn the heat down, to a medium-low and stir
4. Cook the onion for about 20 minutes and if the onions are browning too quickly, turn down the heat and a little splash of water
5. Add the vinegar and let reduce for about 1 minute
6. Remove from the heat and in a medium bowl; combine the caramelized onions and the Greek Yogurt
7. Serve and enjoy your onion dip!

Nutrition Information

Calories: 80, Fat: 4.5g, Carbohydrates: 5g, Dietary Fiber: 1.5g, Protein: 1.5g

Recipe 63: Cheese Dip

(Prep time: 6 Minutes|Cook Time: 5 minutes| Servings: 3)

Ingredients:

- 1.6 Ounces of Cream Cheese
- 1/8 Cup of Butter
- 1 Tablespoon of Heavy Cream
- 1 Tablespoon of mozzarella cheese

Instructions:

1. In a saucepan, place the cream cheese, the butter, and the heavy cream; then place over low heat.
2. Keep stirring until the cheese melts and all your ingredients are very well combined
3. Add in the mozzarella cheese; then whisk very well
4. You can use the sauce immediately or store in the refrigerator

Nutrition Information

Calories: 389, Fat: 39g, Carbohydrates: 2g, Dietary Fiber: 0.4g, Protein: 6g

Recipe 64: Chicken and mayonnaise dip

(Prep time: 6 Minutes|Cook Time: 5 minutes| Servings: 3)

Ingredients:

- ¼ Cup of whole Egg Mayonnaise
- ¼ Cup of sour cream
- 2 Tablespoons of crumbled Feta Crumbled
- 1/3 Tablespoon of Lemon Juice
- 1 Pinch of Pepper
- 1/8 Teaspoon of garlic powder

Instructions:

1. Add all your ingredients to a food processor and blend for about 5 minutes
2. You can add in 2 to 3 tablespoons of hot water if you want a thinner dressing
3. Serve and enjoy!

Nutrition Information

Calories: 138, Fat: 14g, Carbohydrates: 3.5g, Dietary Fiber: 0.5 g, Protein: 3g

Recipe 65: Salad Vinaigrette

(Prep time: 5 Minutes|Cook Time: 0 minutes| Servings: 2-3)

Ingredients:

- ½ cup of extra-virgin olive oil
- 3 tablespoons of vinegar of choice (red wine vinegar, balsamic vinegar, white wine vinegar, red wine vinegar)
- 1 tablespoon of Dijon mustard
- 1 tablespoon of maple syrup or honey
- 2 medium pressed or minced garlic cloves
- ¼ teaspoon of fine sea salt, to taste
- 1 Pinch of freshly ground black pepper, to taste

Instructions:

1. In a liquid measuring bowl, combine all of your ingredients; then stir very well with a whisk
2. Thin out with a little bit of olive oil or balance all the flavours with more maple syrup or more olive oil
3. You can add 1 pinch of salt or vinegar
4. Whisk very well to blend
5. Serve and enjoy immediately!

Nutrition Information

Calories: 43, Fat: 4.17g, Carbohydrates: 1.57g, Dietary Fiber: 0 g, Protein: 0.66g

Desserts (~10 recipes)

Recipe 66: Coconut butter dark chocolate bars

(Prep time: 10 Minutes|Cook Time: 5 minutes| Servings: 6)

Ingredients:

- 4 Oz of coconut butter
- ¼ Cup of almond butter
- 1 ½ Tablespoons of swerve sweetener or maple syrup
- ⅛ Teaspoon of salt
- 1 Pinch of cinnamon
- 1 and ½Oz of dark chocolate

Instructions:

1. Start by melting the coconut butter over medium heat until it melts; and stir for about 2 to 4 minutes
2. Add the maple; the nut butter, the cinnamon and combine very well until your ingredients become smooth
3. Adjust the seasoning of the sweetener
4. Pour about 2/3 of your mixture over a pan lined with a parchment paper
5. Add the chocolate to the remaining quantity of the butter mixture and let heat for about 30 additional seconds

6. Spread the obtained mixture into a loaf pan
7. Let your pan chill for about 1 hour
8. Slice and serve your dessert
9. Enjoy!

Nutrition Information

Calories: 113, Fat: 10g, Carbohydrates: 7.5g, Dietary Fiber: 3.5 g, Protein: 3g

Recipe 67: Cinnamon dates cookies

(Prep time: 12 Minutes|Cook Time: 0 minutes| Servings: 6-7)

Ingredients:

- ⅔ Cup of pitted, softened dates
- ⅓ Cup of coconut butter
- ½ Cup of unsweetened applesauce
- ⅓ Cup of organic coconut flour
- ½ Teaspoon of pure vanilla extract
- 1 Pinch of fine-grain sea salt
- 1 Teaspoon of ground cinnamon
- For the topping use;
- 1 Tablespoon of organic coconut sugar
- 1 Teaspoon of ground cinnamon

Instructions:

1. Place the softened dates into a food processor and process your ingredients over a high speed or until it becomes a paste
2. Add the applesauce; the vanilla and process your ingredients together very well
3. Add the salt, the coconut flour, and the cinnamon; then process very well

4. From the obtained dough; make the shape of balls; then place it over a baking sheet
5. Gently flatten the cookies
6. Place the cookies into the refrigerator for about 10 minutes
7. Top the cookies with the coconut sugar
8. Serve and enjoy your cookies!

Nutrition Information

Calories: 82, Fat: 4.2g, Carbohydrates: 11g, Dietary Fiber: 0.6 g, Protein: 1.6g

Recipe 68: Chocolate Truffles

(Prep time: 15 Minutes|Cook Time: 0 minutes| Servings: 7)

Ingredients:

- ¼ Cup of slightly melted coconut manna
- ¼ Cup of cacao powder
- ¼ Cup of water
- 1 Teaspoon of vanilla extract
- 1 Tablespoon of coconut flour
- 1/8 Cup of maple syrup
- To make the Toppings:
- ¼ Cup of melted dark chocolate chips
- ½ Teaspoon of coconut oil
- ¼ Cup of unsweetened shredded coconut; chopped nuts and raw cacao

Instructions:

1. Start by preparing a medium plate and line it with a wax paper.
2. In a large and deep bowl, mix altogether the coconut manna with the cocoa powder and the vanilla extract
3. Add the water, the maple syrup, and the coconut flour; then mix very well
4. Place the bowl into the refrigerator for about 18 minutes or until the chocolate mixture start hardening
5. Use a small scoop to shape chocolate balls and hold it together
6. Make about 10 to 11 chocolate truffles
7. Arrange the coconut balls or truffles over the prepared plate; then place it into the refrigerator to cool for about 10 minutes, meanwhile, melt the chocolate chips and pour in the coconut oil; then mix very well
8. Place the toppings you want into small bowl
9. With toothpicks; roll the chocolate truffles into the toppings
10. Place the coated truffles over a wax paper; then let it chill for about 30 minutes
11. Serve and enjoy your coconut balls!!

Nutrition Information

Calories: 62, Fat: 4.1g, Carbohydrates: 11g, Dietary Fiber: 4.6 g, Protein: 0.8g

Recipe 68: Christmas Log

(Prep time: 10 Minutes|Cook Time: 10 minutes| Servings: 5)

Ingredients

For the cake:

- 1 and ¼ Cups of sugar100 grams of flour
- 5 Large eggs
- 1 Small teaspoon of vanilla sugar
- For the cream:
- 1 Cup of sugar cubes
- ½ Cup of water
- 3 egg yolks
- 1 ½ Cups of unsalted butter
- 1 Cup of dark chocolate
- 3 ml of coffee extract

Instructions:

1. Start by preparing the rolled cake:
2. Work the 4 egg yolks with the vanilla sugar and the sugar; then mix very well

3. When the mixture is creamy, add a whole egg and work the mixture for a few minutes
4. Add the flour little by little, then add the whites and spread the mixture on a rectangular buttered greaseproof dish
5. Put the dish in the oven at a temperature of 400°F/ 200 ° C for 10 minutes
6. Take the dish out of the oven and turn it over on a fairly cold surface but never remove the paper
7. Cover with a tea towel and prepare the buttercream and to do this, melt the sugar in a quantity of water on a low heat and slowly pour the syrup over the egg yolks; don't stop stirring
8. Add the softened butter and mix gently to obtain a smooth cream
9. Remove the baking paper from your cake and spread with the coffee cream
10. Roll the mixture and even out all the ends; and cover with chocolate cream
11. Decorate the log as you wish, then set aside
12. Serve and enjoy your dessert!

Nutrition Information

Calories: 126, Fat: 5g, Carbohydrates: 17g, Dietary Fiber: 1 g, Protein: 1g

Recipe 69: Medjool Dates Pie

(Prep time: 9 Minutes|Cook Time: 5 minutes| Servings: 6)

Ingredients

To make the crust:
- ½ Cup of pitted Medjool dates
- 1 Cup of almonds
- 1 Ounce of black and green melted dark chocolate
- 1 Tablespoon of melted coconut oil
- 1 Pinch of salt

To make the filling:
- 1 Cup of coconut cream
- 3 and ½ ounces of black and green, dark chocolate
- ¼ Cup of coconut oil
- ½ Cup of pitted Medjool dates
- 1 Teaspoon of vanilla extract
- For the toppings:
- 1 Cup of fresh berries
- 1 Cup of whipped coconut cream

Instructions:

1. Soak the dates into warm water for about 10 minutes
2. Pulse the dates and the almonds into a food processor; then add the melted chocolate
3. Add the coconut oil and the salt and process until your ingredients are very well combined
4. Press the mixture of the crust in a baking pie pan
5. Clean the food processor; then heat the coconut cream; the chocolate and the coconut oil and wait until your ingredients become smooth
6. Fill the chocolate mixture into the crust and let it chill for about 1 to 2 hours
7. Top your chocolate pie with the whipped coconut cream and the fresh fruits
8. Serve and enjoy your pie!

Nutrition Information

Calories: 96, Fat: 8g, Carbohydrates: 5g, Dietary Fiber: 1 g, Protein: 1.3g

Recipe 71: Healthy Dark Chocolate Cake

(Prep time: 10 Minutes|Cook Time: 40 minutes| Servings: 5-6)

Ingredients

For the wet ingredients

- ¼ Cup coconut oil, melted
- 3 Large pasteurized eggs
- ¼ Cup maple syrup, pure
- 1 Cup orange juice, freshly squeezed
- 1 Large orange, zest
- ¼ cup almond milk, unsweetened

For the chocolate glaze:

- 4 Oz chocolate bar, 85% dark

For the dry ingredients:

- 1 ½ Cups almond flour, finely packed
- ⅓ cup coconut flour sifted
- 1 Pinch salt
- 1 tsp baking soda

For the garnish

- 1 orange, only zest

Instructions:

1. Preheat an oven to about 350° F
2. Line an 8x4 inch baking pan with a parchment paper and set it aside
3. Combine the almond flour with the coconut flour, salt and baking soda in a large mixing bowl and mix
4. Now, combine the maple syrup with the eggs, the orange juice and the almond milk in a separate bowl and make sure the coconut oil is melted; then add it to the mixture
5. Whisk the wet ingredients very well; then add the dry ingredients you have placed in a separate bowl to the wet ingredients and combine everything
6. Pour the batter into the loaf pan and make sure to spread it out nicely on top
7. Bake for about 40 minutes in your preheated oven
8. Remove the pan from the oven and set it aside to cool for about 5 minutes; in the meantime, make the dark chocolate glaze by adding the dark chocolate bar by bringing a pot to a boil; then toss the chocolate into a small bowl and place the bowl in the water; stir from time to time until the chocolate becomes smooth
9. Pour the batter over the loaf pan and evenly spread it on top
10. Top with the orange zest; then slice the cake
11. Serve and enjoy your delicious cake!

Nutrition Information

Calories: 222, Fat: 20.3g, Carbohydrates: 7.9g, Dietary Fiber: 3.3 g, Protein: 7g

Recipe 72: Macadamia cookies

(Prep time: 8 Minutes|Cook Time: 15 minutes| Servings: 8)

Ingredients:

- 1/2 cup coconut oil, melted
- 2 tablespoons almond butter
- 1 egg
- 1 1/2 cup almond flour
- 2 tablespoons unsweetened cocoa powder
- 1/2 cup granulated erythritol sweetener
- 1 teaspoon vanilla extract
- 1/2 teaspoon baking soda
- 1/4 cup chopped macadamia nuts
- 1 Pinch of salt

Instructions:

1. Start by preheating your oven to a temperature of about 350°F.
2. Combine the almond butter with the coconut oil, the almond flour, the cocoa powder, the swerve, the vanilla extract, the baking soda, the chopped macadamia nut and the salt in a large mixing bowl
3. Mix your ingredients very well with a fork or a spoon; then set it aside

4. Line a cookie sheet with a parchment paper or just grease it very well
5. Drop small balls of about 1 ½ inches wide; then gently flatten the cookies with your hands
6. Bake your cookies for about 15 minutes; then remove it from the oven and set it aside to cool for about 10 minutes
7. Serve and enjoy your macadamia cookies!

Nutrition Information

Calories: 130, Fat: 10g, Carbohydrates: 6g, Dietary Fiber: 4g, Protein: 6g

Recipe 73: Cocoa Myffins

(Prep time: 7 Minutes|Cook Time: 20 minutes| Servings: 7)

Ingredients:

- 1 ¼ Cups of Almond Flour
- ½ Cup of cocoa powder, unsweetened Cocoa Powder
- ½ cup of Erythritol
- 1 and ½ Teaspoons of Baking Powder
- 1 teaspoon of pure Vanilla Extract
- 3 Large eggs
- 2/3 Cup of heavy cream
- 3 Ounces of melted almond butter
- ½ Cup of Chocolate Chips

Instructions:

1. Preheat your oven to a temperature of about 350°F.
2. In a large bowl, combine the almond flour with the cocoa powder, the erythritol, and the baking powder and mix very well
3. Add in the vanilla extract, the eggs, and the heavy cream and mix very well.
4. Add in the melted coconut oil and mix again
5. Add in the sugar-free chocolate chips to your ingredients and stir very well.

6. Line a muffin tray with cupcake papers
7. Spoon your prepared mixture into the 12 holes of a standard muffin tray or any muffin tray you have
8. Bake your muffins for about 20 minutes
9. Remove the muffins from the oven and let cool for 5 minutes
10. Serve and enjoy your delicious muffins!

Nutrition Information

Calories: 112, Fat: 9g, Carbohydrates: 4g, Dietary Fiber: 2g, Protein: 5.8g

Recipe 75: Lava Cake

(Prep time: 10 Minutes|Cook Time: 10 minutes| Servings: 3-4)

Ingredients:

- 2 Oz of dark chocolate; you should at least use chocolate of 85% cocoa solids
- 1 Tablespoon of super-fine almond flour
- 2 Oz of unsalted almond butter
- 2 Large eggs, beaten

Instructions:

1. Heat your oven to a temperature of about 350° Fahrenheit.
2. Grease 2 heatproof ramekins with almond butter.
3. Now, melt the chocolate and the almond butter and stir very well
4. Beat the eggs very well with a mixer
5. Add the eggs to the chocolate and the butter mixture and mix very well with almond flour and the swerve; then stir
6. Pour the dough into 2 ramekins
7. Bake for about 9 to 10 minutes

8. Serve and enjoy your cakes!

Nutrition Information

Calories: 237.5, Fat: 18g, Carbohydrates: 12.6g, Dietary Fiber: 8.3g, Protein: 4.5g

Concluding Chapter

Welcome to this Thanksgiving Cookbook that has been designed only to help you learn how to best celebrate Thanksgiving with your family offering you a large array of recipes that will make your cooking experience better. This cookbook is packed with recipes that are at the same time healthy and mesmerizing so that you can cook like a master cook during Thanksgiving and spend a more enjoyable time with your family and beloved ones.

You might wonder how is it possible to cook a large menu made of different categories of meals on a happy and familial occasion like Thanksgiving. And if you are afraid that you won't be able to have your meals ready on time; after reading this cookbook you will be able to change your mind and you will get an opportunity to enjoy some of the best recipes you can ever stumble into.

So if you want to find an answer to the main secrets and learn how you bake as many sumptuous recipes as possible; then you have come to the right place and you have picked the right choice. In this book; you will find all the cooking tips you need to know so that you can come up with a wonderful dish everyone won't be able to forget its taste.

From main dishes; to different types of sides, desserts, dips, snacks, and even more; this cookbook will make a great addition to your bookshelf and will make a perfect gift for your sister, mother, daughter, and everyone who loves cooking with love. Indeed; learning to cook won't be difficult as you imagine it can be with a book.

You might think that I am exaggerating, but once you start reading this cookbook you will discover that I will offer you what any other books didn't offer you, which is the combination of some of your favorite ingredients like chocolate, strawberries, fruits, and even candies, but all in a healthy way.

And if you are a beginner in the culinary world; you don't need to worry because this cookbook will help you learn different types of delicious recipes that you can enjoy no matter which diet you are following. Indeed, this cookbook includes recipes that everyone will like and that are healthy for all types of diets; everyone will find a recipe they will adore in this book.

And in addition to the wide variety of recipes, you will find in this cookbook, you will also discover many precious pieces of information about thanksgiving; its history, and the background this happy special occasion that unites all the families in the entire world. This cookbook will not only help you enjoy a wonderful Thanksgiving with your family and beloved ones, but it will also teach you cooking with all types of affordable ingredients.

In this cookbook, you will also find combined with the recipe pre-calculated nutrition information that will help you govern your calorie intake. Moreover, you will learn and get to experience that thanksgiving can be a more enjoyable experience more than an exhausting one that deprives you of sitting with your family and enjoy your time with your beloved people. In this book, you will find:

- The history of thanksgiving
- Types of foods and thanksgiving traditions
- Cooking measurements and general tips
- A wide range of delicious recipes including:
    - *Lava Cake*
    - *Cocoa Myffins*
    - *Macadamia cookies*
    - *Christmas Log*
    - *Chicken and Cheese Soup*
    - *Baked Barramundi with olives*
    - *Salmon with orange juice*
    - *Stuffed Turkey*
    - *Roasted Turkey*
    - *Cola Ham*
    - *Fried Turkey breasts*

References:

- ~ 201410.1001/jama.2013.279860JAMA
- ~ Vignettes: Thanksgiving Advisory
- ~ 199410.1126/science.266.5188.1262Science
- ~ 1855Lucy Larcom10.2307/25526995The Crayon
- ~ 1873E. E. Hale10.2307/20636647The Aldine
- ~ 1989David Ray10.2307/377712College English
- ~ 184710.1038/scientificamerican11271847-74Scientific American
- ~ 198710.1177/105345128702300211Academic Therapy
- ~ Eugene Merrill - Qumran and predestination – 1975
- ~ Thanksgiving—Intercession—Thanksgiving: Col. 1:3-14
- ~ Peter O'brien - Introductory Thanksgivings in the Letters of Paul - 1977
- ~ Thanksgiving Day: A Speech at a Royal Albert Hall Concert in celebration of American Thanksgiving Day November 23, 1944
- ~ The Dawn of Liberation : War Speeches
- ~ Thanksgiving Sermon by Absalom Jones (1808)
- ~ African American Studies Center - 2012
- ~ Priorclave Provided - protocols.io – 2015
- ~ The Thanksgiving Book: A Companion to the Holiday Covering Its History, Lore, Traditions, Foods, and Symbols, Including Primary Sources, Poems, Prayers, Songs, Hymns, and Recipes, Supplemented by a Chronology, Bibliography with Web Sites and Index200917Laurie C. Hillstrom. The Thanksgiving Book: A Companion to the Holiday Covering Its History, Lore, Traditions, Foods, and Symbols, Including Primary Sources, Poems, Prayers, Songs, Hymns, and Recipes, Supplemented by a Chronology, Bibliography with Web Sites and Index. Detroit, MI: Omnigraphics 2008. xi + 328 pp., ISBN: 978 0 7808 0403 6 $65
- ~ 2009Lara Ursin Cummings10.1108/09504120910925616Reference Reviews
Thanksgiving
201410.1001/jama.2013.279860JAMA
U.S.$44.50 (cloth), 735 pp. (Numerical Recipes Example Book (C), U.S.$19.95; Numerical Recipes C Diskette, U.S.$29.95; Numerical Recipes Example Diskette (C), U.S.$24.95; Numerical Recipes FORTRAN Diskette for Macintosh, U.S.$39.95; Numerical Recipes Pascal Diskette for Macintosh, U.S.$39.95; Numerical Recipes Example Diskette (FORTRAN) for Macintosh, U.S.$29.95; Numerical Recipes Example Diskette (Pascal) for Macintosh, U.S.$29.95.)W.H. Press, B.P. Flannery, S.A. Teukolsky and W.T. Vetterling, Numerical Recipes in C: The Art of Scientific Computing, Cambridge University Press, Princeton, NJ (1988)
- ~ 1990L ROPER10.1016/s0092-8240(05)80365-9Bulletin of Mathematical Biology
Vignettes: Thanksgiving Advisory
199410.1126/science.266.5188.1262Science

- 1855Lucy Larcom10.2307/25526995The Crayon
  Thanksgiving Days
- 1873E. E. Hale10.2307/20636647The Aldine
  Thanksgiving
  1989David Ray10.2307/377712College English
- Thanksgiving
  184710.1038/scientificamerican11271847-74Scientific American
- Thanksgiving Thoughts
  198710.1177/105345128702300211Academic Therapy
  A Veteran's Thanksgiving
  1937Senex10.1136/bmj.2.4014.1201-aBMJ

CPSIA information can be obtained
at www.ICGtesting.com
Printed in the USA
LVHW010552180722
723709LV00008B/568